The Angler's Library

COD FISHING

BOB GLEDHILL

BARRIE & JENKINS
COMMUNICA - EUROPA

First published in 1978 by
Barrie & Jenkins Ltd
24 Highbury Crescent, London N5 1RX

ISBN: 0 214 20556 8

*Printed in Great Britain by
The Anchor Press Ltd and bound by
Wm Brendon & Son Ltd, both of
Tiptree, Essex*

The Angler's Library

COD FISHING

The Angler's Library

Contents

Introduction

Why write a book on cod fishing? For one reason it's the aim of more rod hours than any other sea fish. That's fact. It isn't the most commonly caught type of sea fish—flatties take that honour—but cod comes a good second place. However, if we consider the number of rod hours against the number caught, that statistic shows either a lack of cod, a lack of understanding, or a little bit of both. The hard truth is that there are more blank cod fishing trips than successful ones, so there's my reason.

I have not written the book with the raw beginner in mind, but have assumed that the reader has already gained a rudimentary knowledge of the basic skills and simply wants to try to learn where he has been going adrift in his quest for the cod.

One of the lovely things about fishing is that so little can be proved or disproved conclusively. Events can lead you to assume something but you can never know for certain whether an idea is the best or the most effective. Only a fish knows that. So writing about fishing can never be anything but one person's opinions, assumptions and experience. The following pages are mine.

Most important—after you have read this book, do not believe that what you have read is the only way to catch cod. There are dozens of ways, but many of them peculiar to one particular bit of coastline. If I listed them all (and I surely don't know them all) the book would be far too long, far too boring and far too expensive. What I have done is to outline basic, blueprint styles that can easily be adapted to suit a particular circumstance.

Always remember that it's your own experience that best tells you how to catch fish, not any written word. But what the printed page can do is to stimulate ideas, suggest different approaches and explain how anglers in a different part of the country catch the same fish you are after.

The first time cod came into my life was at the tender age of twelve. We had a geography teacher whom the whole class disliked because of his habit of walking up and down the rows of desks and asking obscure and difficult questions. If one didn't know the answer, or got it wrong, he would dust the back of the unfortunate scholar's head with his hand. We called him Flipper because of that.

One day Flipper came up behind me and dug a boney finger into my shoulder. "You, boy . . . how many eggs does a female cod lay?" I racked my adolescent brain for the answer. Hens laid one at a time, I thought, I knew seagulls laid three, perhaps cod were similar to seagulls as they both lived in the sea.

"P-p-please, sir . . . three?"

Whack! "Foolish boy. A female cod lays five million eggs. If every one survived you could walk to America on the back of codfish after five years."

A female cod does produce something in the order of five million eggs, but looking back I'm not so sure about Flipper's assumption that after five years you could walk to America on them. However, the presence of cod was forcefully driven home to me and to this day I can recall the vivid mental picture I had of stepping onto the base of the Statue of Liberty off the back of a grey Atlantic cod.

Flipper no doubt based his idea on not only all the five million eggs surviving, but all growing at a remarkable rate with no trawling to interfere with them.

If you believe that trawling affects only offshore fisheries and that the small inshore boats do little if any damage to fish stocks, talk to someone who remembers rod and line fishing in the years between 1945 and 1948. Six years of world war had kept trawling down to a bare minimum and the cod had a chance to grow without interference, showing what stocks were like a couple of hundred years ago. It only took the trawling industry three years to get the level of fish stocks down to its pre-war level, but those halcyon years showed what cod fishing sport could be like if the cod wasn't a fish that was so suited to a jacket of batter.

The great tragedy about cod trawling is the size limit. Logically, the size limit should be after the first spawning year. This way, although the cod is trawled up, it has had a chance to replace itself. This is the way size limits are operated with that other highly commercial fish, the plaice, which spawns at nine inches and can be trawled at ten inches.

Even a fast-growing cod will be 4 lb. before it is sexually

mature, and think how many cod under that size are trawled up. And dare I suggest that anglers take more immature fish than mature fish?

This may have seemed a melancholy introduction to something which can give so much pleasure, and there's nothing anglers can do about it, but it had to be said. However, I promise no more frowns for the rest of the book.

Cod—the fish and how it works

It is not necessary to know much about the biology of the cod to be able to catch them on rod and line. But I think most anglers who have bought this book must have a degree of curiosity about the make-up of the fish.

The distribution of cod in the British Isles is governed largely by the temperature of the sea. Most cod are found in sea temperatures ranging from one to five degrees Centigrade. They will tolerate up to ten degrees or as low as freezing point, but water of minus two degrees Centigrade is lethal. In practical terms this explains why in Scotland, part of Northern England and most offshore areas (where despite air temperature, the sea temperature remains cool), cod can be taken all the year round.

The age of sexual maturity of the cod varies widely. The dense shoals of spawning cod that descend upon the Lofoten Islands off the North West coast of Norway every spring can be anything from eight to 12 years old before they mature. This is a direct result of poor feeding. Around the shores of Great Britain, where the feeding is good, cod can be as young as two or three years when they mature.

The amount of eggs a female cod produces (called the fecundity) ranges from two to ten million. During spawning, the male cod releases his sperm at the same time as the female releases the eggs, with the movement of the water and the fish mixing the two.

It is obviously an inefficient method of propagation, but in areas where the spawning cod are tightly packed, sperm and eggs from many fish will mix. After spawning the eggs float freely for a couple of weeks before rising to the surface. In this initial stage mortality of the young is incredibly high because of predation and the destructive force of heavy seas.

It has never been proved that a heavy spawning means a higher level of survival for the young cod; in fact the reverse

9

may be true. With a heavy spawning the predatory fish may become completely preoccupied with feeding on cod spawn, and leave the spawn of other fish completely alone. So if, say, cod and coalfish spawn over the same ground and the coalfish spawning is very heavy and the cod very light, the coalfish spawn may be decimated and the cod spawn left alone.

The amount of food available when the eggs hatch is also critical. After the young cod has eaten the yolk-sac it must have an immediate supply of the right sort of planktonic food. If there is a shortage of this food, mass mortality will again follow. The warm spring sun brings with it a plankton bloom in the upper layers of the ocean where the eggs hatch, which is why cod spawn in the spring.

After three to five months the cod fry are between three and six centimetres long and descend to the sea bed to begin their demersal life. The growth rate of cod varies with the quality of the feeding. Rich, inshore waters provide a much higher growth rate than deeper, offshore areas. The average growth rate for inshore cod is shown in Figure 1.

GROWTH RATE SCALE FOR COD						
AGE IN YEARS	1	2	3	4	5	6
Average length in cms.	18	36	55	68	78	89
Length increase in cms.	18	19	13	10	11	—
Percentage increase	100	52	23	14	14	—

FIG. 1.

There seems to be an agreement among sea anglers that cod spawn better in colder winters. The freeze-up of 1963 and the subsequent good cod fishing of the mid-sixties is cited as a classic example. Yet I have never heard of any evidence other than very circumstantial to support this cold-weather hypothesis. It is true that 1963 was a very good spawning year, but so were the following three years, and that run of good spawnings followed a period from 1958 to 1963 when spawnings were poor.

I have already said that there is no evidence from fishery research to suggest that the level of egg production or level of fertilised eggs has any bearing whatsoever on the final numbers of cod that survive.

The good cod fishing of the mid-sixties is far more likely to be attributable to the four-year good spell for spawn survival from 1963 to 1966 than to a freak winter of one year. There would be a noticeable drop in rod and line catches after that period as there then followed three bad years for spawning.

The evidence for my hypothesis that cold weather has no proven bearing on cod stocks comes from information provided by the Marine Laboratory of the Department of Agriculture and Fisheries for Scotland at Aberdeen, who also told me that other recent good spawning years were 1969, 1970, 1974 and 1976.

I trust that the ghost of the winter of '63 has been laid to rest.

Many of the statistics on cod fecundity and growth that form the basis of study today comes from the pioneering work of Michael Graham, who in the 1920s–40s made extensive studies of cod from the North Sea. His growth rate figures were $3\frac{1}{4}$ in. in six months, 6–7 in. after one year, 10 in. after one and a half years, 14 in. after two years, 17 in. after two and a half years, and 22 in. after three years.

Figures published in the late 1960s by the Ministry of Agriculture, Fisheries and Food of cod growth in the Irish Sea were: one year, 8 in. (4 oz.); one and a half years, 12 in. ($\frac{3}{4}$ lb.); two years, 16 in. ($1\frac{1}{2}$ lb.); three years, 20 in. ($2\frac{1}{2}$ lb.).

Thirty years of research has done nothing to invalidate Michael Graham's work or to show any appreciable change in the growth rate of cod despite a considerable reduction in numbers.

Figure 2 shows the basic construction of the cod with its characteristic three dorsal fins, protruding upper jaw and the barbel underneath the lower jaw. That barbel is a vital sense organ of taste as well as touch. Taste organs are also located on parts of the head as well as in the mouth.

The lateral line, which runs distinctly from the gill cover to the tail, is a row of tiny sense organs which divide into branches on the head. The lateral line works like sonar, with the fish sending and receiving signals. This echo-sounding ability enables the fish to fix the position of stationary objects around it, an obvious essential when living in wrecks or on broken ground. Furthermore, the lateral line is also able to pick up the pressure waves given off by moving objects such

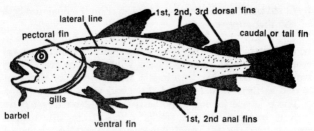

FIG. 2. External characteristics of a cod.

as small fish or a lure, and certainly the noise and vibration from propeller blades.

Cod vary in colour from a yellow-grey to deep red according to the ground on which they are taken from. The native cod which live permanently among weeds and rock adopt the easily recognisable reddish colour, while those that live over sandy areas, or in deep water have the grey colour.

The colour is nothing to do with feeding habits (i.e. the idea that red cod are that colour through feeding on red crabs), but is caused by a reaction through the nervous system whereby the pigmentary colour cells group together in such a way as to *appear* a certain colour.

However, interesting as ecology and biology are, it is the catching of cod that we are concerned with, so I'll get down to the nuts and bolts of cod fishing . . . the tackle.

CHAPTER ONE

Cod Fishing Tackle

There are three basic approaches to cod fishing from the shore: light line and distance, close-range rock and weed fishing, and a middle-of-the-road mixture of the two. Which style you adopt depends entirely on the ground you are going to fish on, you cannot have much choice if you want maximum effectiveness for your efforts. You may catch fish with heavy rock gear on a clear shingle beach, just as you may get a fish out of dense weed and rock with 16 lb. line but the only thing that would prove is that anything is possible in fishing, and most of us know that already.

You must not take your adopted style to every place you go. There was a time when I ridiculed the 60 lb. line and Scarborough centre-pin tackle still so popular in Yorkshire and Durham. I argued that the 30 lb. line was the most any forward-thinking shore angler should have to use, no matter what the conditions. I argued that if you got stuck round a rock or in a kelp stalk it wouldn't matter if the line was 150 lb. you would lose it, so why go heavier than 30 lb.?

That was arrogance spawned from ignorance. After I began to fish Yorkshire and Durham more, some of the really hard rock marks such as Flamborough Head and St Mary's Island at Whitley Bay were opened up to me by anglers who have fished this type of ground all their lives. I then realised my earlier foolishness. Heavy gear is essential. Obstructions that won't budge with a 30 lb. line will with a 50 lb. line. It's as simple as that.

I don't like travelling for its own sake, but I do enjoy fishing different beaches, so it is inevitable that many of the venues I fish demand long casting. If you believe casting a long way for cod is a myth perpetuated by the tackle trade and an élitist few tournament casters, go down to a beach where distance casting is claimed to be vital and see how your 60 yards fares against 120 yards. You might drop lucky and find the fish close in one night, but you don't have to fish these beaches for long to learn that long casting is a vital key to success.

13

Still with distance, it is puzzling why so few shore anglers really bother about their casting technique since it has such a profound effect on the amount of cod you catch. Yet it only takes a few hours with proper instruction to reach what to some are telephone number distances. Only when you want to push leads beyond the 160 yard mark does it begin to get really hard work. The only things you need to cast a long way are a correctly balanced and loaded rod and reel, an understanding of technique, and the patience to practise for a few hours a week.

I mentioned middle-of-the-road style of cod fishing by which I mean ground with a beach of stones, perhaps mussels, and a few patches of weed. Lines of 14 lb. to 16 lb. that are suitable for sand would break too easily on this mixed ground. But neither do you need the extreme of a Scarborough and 60 lb. line. You want something in between the two which is why I called it middle-of-the-road. Lines between 25 lb. and 35 lb.

To be equipped for all three types of beaches, ideally you need two rods. One designed for casting, the kind most tackle shops sell, and a much more rigid, possibly shorter weed rod that won't have too soft an action when used with very heavy lines. In practice, as most cod anglers tend to stick to their own area, you can manage with just one of the two types, unless you wish to fish two rods at a time in which case you double up on everything.

How do you tell a good casting rod? The qualities you are searching for are stiffness, so that the rod can absorb all the compression you can put into it; lightness, so that it isn't heavy to hold and heavy to throw; and sensitivity so the tip will register bites clearly.

Ideally, the length of the rod should be that which suits your individual casting style, and that can be anything between 11 ft. 6 in. and 14 ft. There are some anglers who believe that the longer the rod, the further the cast, and so will always look for the longest rod possible. In fact long rods can be a handicap in getting extra distance with some styles. If you stick to a true Pendulum style of casting, you should find that 12 ft. is too long for this very fast style. Actually, my Pendulum rod is 11 ft. 5 in.

The problem is that most anglers do not cast true fixed styles, instead giving their own variation on established styles so you cannot fix rigid lengths for rods. If you cast with an overhead sweep—as a great many anglers do—almost certainly a rod of around 13 ft. will give you the greater distance. If you drag the lead from the floor (South African), as a small number do, then a rod of 14 ft. will give you greater distance, and if you have a cast that is a mixture of two styles then your ideal rod length will be something in between.

The reason, incidentally, that so many production rods are two equal 6 ft. lengths is nothing to do with the fishing or casting ability of the rod but that is the best length the tackle trade has found for selling. Without argument, the best way of buying a fishing rod is to have one made up that suits your casting style in both length and position of reel fittings, but there are very few firms or tackle dealers prepared to sell rods in this way. That is the reason why all my rods were built by me. They may not look much but I believe they are unbeatable for my casting and fishing styles.

The glass I used is Cono-Flex, built by Carroll McManus, in my mind by far the most superior surfcasting blank designers in the world. All my rod rings are Diamite, expensive but again the best there is. They never groove and are immensely strong, resisting breakage no matter how many times they are banged and dropped.

The firm Magnum Rods sell Cono-Flex surf blanks in kit form, and the next time you want a new rod I recommend them to you, making the final length the one that suits you.

If you still want to buy a standard production rod, beware of some of the claims made by some manufacturers for their rods. All claim great distances for their products and bewilder the angler with the claims made for them. A top-flight tournament caster has a powerful technique that will send a lead a long way irrespective of which rod he uses. I wouldn't be surprised to see a tournament caster whip three rings on a yard brush and cast it 100 yards. That is not an insult to those personalities who have put their name to a particular rod; far from it. I'm just saying beware of advertising copywriters and never think you can buy distance from a tackle shop. The right rod helps you, but yards come from technique rather than from the rod.

If you want a rod for very heavy rock fishing to use with a Scarborough reel it must be made from very strong glass to withstand the strains very heavy line strengths impose on a rod. A length of about 11 ft. is ideal and the reel fitting has to be at the bottom of the rod. On my weed rod I have fitted unusually wide rings so that if I pick weed up on the line it has less chance of jamming round a ring. The tip of my weed rod is about as thick again as a conventional beach rod, about the thickness you would find a foot below the tip.

To summarise on the choice of rod: for normal fishing you want a rod 11 ft. 6 in. to 14 ft. long, light, stiff and capable of absorbing all the compression you can give it. Avoid sloppy, soft rods, if anything err on the side of rigidity. If you plan to fish very rough ground with heavy lines, go for a shorter rod with a very stiff action, almost unbending.

Reels

Matching the right reel for the rod is again a matter of looking at the type of fishing you are going to do. Think how far you will want to cast, what sort of breaking strain line you will need and if there are any special qualities you want. Special qualities beyond what you would normally expect from a reel are things like high retrieve rate for fishing over very broken ground where you want the tackle to plane up from the bottom as soon as possible, or maybe a high capacity for fishing flat sandy beaches where you are backing up with tide and having to pay out line as you back up the beach. The three types of reel you can choose from are the multiplier, the fixed spool and the centre-pin.

Multipliers

Considering the number of people who have problems with casting a multiplier it's a wonder they have remained as popular as they are. Against the multiplier is its intolerance of jerky casting, resulting in over-runs; its retrieve rate which for many models is below the fixed spool and the centre-pin; and the cost, which with imported multipliers continues to go through the roof. The two things in their favour are their ability to outcast the other two types of reel and the ease of handling that comes from a smooth-running compact reel.

To understand how an over-run occurs, put the spool out of gear and give a sharp tug at the line. The spool will throw the line up in coils until it jams round itself, maybe throwing the spool into reverse. This is your classic over-run situation. You can stop over-runs happening by tightening up the spindle bearing on the side plate. This certainly works but won't do the reel much good, and will cause the spindle to wear, the bearing to wear, or both.

A far more efficient way of stopping over-runs is to learn to cast so smoothly that the spool only releases as much line as is required by the lead. However, casting smoothly is something that takes quite a bit of practice. The compromise is to slow the spindle down with lubricants, though I'll go into that later.

Going back to the business of the line discharging from the reel at the same rate as the weight is demanding it: the discharge rate will obviously alter according to the size of the spool. If you attempt to cast a long way with a large diameter spool, too much line will come off. This is one of the reasons why small multipliers allow you to cast further than very big ones.

Gravitational pull is the main cause of a weight ceasing to travel upwards and away from you. The power you pass from your muscles into the rod (compression) is transmitted into the weight and this power propels the lead. The force in the lead just after casting is greater than the downward force of gravity, so the lead resists the force of gravity. But when the amount of force in the lead becomes less, gravity forces the lead earthwards. Not only does gravity slow the lead down, but as more power from the lead is lost, so its speed decreases and the demand it makes from the reel lessens. Because at the end of the cast the demand is less, you might get an obvious over-run there, with the spool spewing line off, but the weight not taking it.

Two things happen to prevent that. First, the gravitational pull that slows the lead down also slows the spool down. Spin a bicycle wheel and eventually it will stop without anything touching it. That is gravity at work. The second factor is that as more and more line comes off the reel, the amount discharged per revolution lessens as the depth of line on the reel decreases. Look at Figure 3 to see what I mean.

See also that the decrease in depth on a wide spool is so much less than that on a narrow spool reel, consequently you are more likely to get an over-run with a wide spool reel than with a narrow one.

So, on choosing a multiplier for smooth, long casting, look for a narrow spool, smaller-than-average model. If you're using a reel like that, at least you know it's you that is to blame for your over-runs and not the tools you are working with.

Several manufacturers produce reels in this specification, though the only ones I recommend through experience are the Abu 6000 and 6500 ranges. These two are standard equipment on the tournament field, which must say something. There could be other reels of this type that perform well, but I cannot recommend what I haven't used.

It invariably follows that long casting (and a reel suited to it) is needed over flat, clear ground, where there are few, if any, obstacles. This allows you to use light breaking strain lines, which in turn are more supple and will help you cast

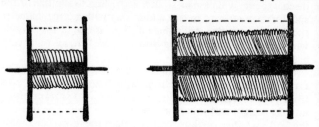

FIG. 3. This illustrates the depth of line on a spool before and after a cast. The broken rule explains that the demand for line by the weight lessens towards the end of the cast, but if line is still coming from the reel at a similar speed as when the weight first started travelling, that extra line will bunch up into an over-run. The discharge per revolution of the spool lessens as the depth of line on the spool decreases. This illustrates why wide spool reels are more prone to over-run trouble than narrow ones.

further. Reels in this small class I load with 12 lb. or 17 lb. breaking strain. My reason for choosing these particular strengths is a simple one: the manufacturer who makes the line I use has a limited range and these two come nearest to the upper and lower limit I use on small multipliers.

Less than a 12 lb. line and even on the cleanest of beaches you could be troubled by frequent breakages. Not from cod, but from, say, a build-up of weed on the line, anchor prongs digging into mud or sand, or the odd stone getting in the way. Also, remember that while it may say 12 lb. on the label, by the time you have knotted it, stretched it, wetted it, it will be substantially less.

On slightly stony ground, when there is some weed floating about, or any other condition that would give me cause for concern with the 12 lb. line, I change spools and use the 17 lb. line. If I wanted to use a heavier line than that, I change to a larger reel.

On ground that is mixed to rough, small multipliers are not recommended on a number of counts. You will certainly wish to use heavier line than 17 lb. to withstand pulling out of obstacles. Heavier line will put greater stresses on the reel than there should be; the small handle and turning circle of these reels doesn't allow you much leverage; with greater line diameter the capacity of the small reel is cut back; and the biggest problem of all is the retrieve rate of a small reel. Don't think of the return ratio but the true line recovery rate. Over rough ground you want to get the weight off the bottom —or at least to skim it instead of dragging along it—as soon as possible. This is why line recovery rate is so important when choosing a large capacity reel.

Which to choose? Consider the jobs the reel will have to do before you decide. First, it still has to allow you to cast a weight a reasonable distance. Maybe not so far as the small multiplier, but still capable of punching out a bait. For this reason spool lightness counts, so heavy metal spools are out, and light alloy, nylon and plastic are in. A further major job is line recovery, for the reasons already stated. Robustness of construction and reliability are economic considerations.

In the medium to high capacity category there are dozens of models to choose from. Abu, Penn, Mitchell, Gladding, Shakespeare, and a few more manufacturers, all have a wide choice of multipliers in this bracket. To choose which one is suited to you, think about casting, retrieve and reliability and see how each model fares.

As far as casting goes, there isn't as much difference between each model as you might think. If you have the basic ability to cast a long way, you can do it with most well-made reels. The only one that stands out particularly from the crowd is the Abu 7000.

When it comes to retrieve rate, the differences really begin to show. If you accept my previous argument in favour of reels with a higher retrieve rate you can put capacity multipliers in exact numerical order as all manufacturers declare in their sales literature the retrieve ratio of their reels.

I think there is a case for marketing a reel with a 5 : 1 ratio, higher than anything I've ever come across. The basic design problem with a high ratio is that when bringing a heavy weight in, it becomes harder work to reel in, both for the angler and the reel. Perhaps manufacturers are worried that their reels sacrifice so much for lightness that they haven't any spare strength left for robustness. Until the day of the 5 : 1 reel comes, the highest recovery rate with a full spool, of reels suitable for shorecasting, will continue to be the Abu 9000C which with its 4.2 : 1 return ratio and a full spool of line can bring in over twenty inches of line per revolution.

Close behind comes a reel that hasn't the popularity it deserves, the Penn 501 Jigmaster. This is a narrow spool version of the more well-known Jigmaster 500 and has a ratio of 4 : 1 that brings line in only marginally less than the Abu 9000C. The Abu 7000 weighs in with a ratio of 4.06 : 1 but the smaller spool puts it behind the first two. There is then a gaggle of reels between 3 : 1 and 4 : 1. Anything less than 3 : 1 I wouldn't use. When you think of line recovery rates remember that when you've hardly any line left on a reel, each revolution of the spool pulls in much less than a full spool, and manufacturers' claims for recovery rate are probably based on a full spool, which the moment you cast out you haven't got.

The last quality to look for in a capacity shorecasting reel is the robustness and reliability of it. Not only in construction of the cage and cogs do you want something workmanlike, but particularly so in the spool. The three most common materials are alloy, nylon and plastic. Alloy spools, as fitted to the Abu range, I have no complaints about. The weight is minimal and I have never had one shatter. The same cannot be said for either nylon or plastic. Nylon is claimed to be shatterproof but it isn't. If you wind on under enough pressure (and there are times when it is unavoidable), you will run the risk of proving the manufacturers' claims wrong. You might get a new spool for your trouble, but you could have had a day's fishing ruined by a break.

The plastic spools fitted to Penn reels are poor. There is no other word to describe them in my opinion. An otherwise excellent reel is let down on this one count. I, like a great many other anglers, first learnt to love (and occasionally hate) the multiplier with the help of Penn reels. But I've lost count of the number of spools I've shattered after reeling in under stress.

For general construction and quality of materials I think Penn shine out bright and clear. I've a Penn Squidder that is fifteen years old and the only thing that has ever gone wrong with it (apart from those spools) is that the torpedo handle broke off. For many years I never used anything but that Squidder, and although it's looking worn these days, mechanically it is still good.

On general construction I think Abu are not all they could be. Just before the red 9000 was phased out to make way for its black replacement, the 9000C, I heard several complaints about bad corrosion on the alloy side plates. With brass plates, the 9000C has overcome this problem, but that thin alloy is still used for the smaller Ambassadeur reels, and I've a 6000C that is badly pitted. Another fault of the 9000C is the anti-reverse dog, which wears far too quickly. The result with a faulty anti-reverse dog is that the reel spins backwards in gear, which apart from anything else can give unwary knuckles a severe rap.

I don't use Mitchell multipliers, though a friend who uses nothing but these reels tells me that there are anti-reverse dog problems with this reel. General construction of the Mitchell reels is sound.

I could now give a best-buy paragraph and plug away for the reels I use, but having spelt out the qualities looked for, and the qualities offered, it shouldn't be too much of a hard job to find the one to suit your fishing.

I load the capacity reels with either 28 lb. or 35 lb. breaking strain line. The 28 lb. is for stony, broken ground, or maybe fishing over mussels or medium weed beds where there are too many breakages from getting fastened up on the bottom to use anything much lighter. The 35 lb. breaking strain is for really rough ground—thick weed and boulders. With any heavier line than that I use a Scarborough centre-pin.

Maintenance is something that hasn't a great bearing on the amount of cod you catch, but it does affect the life span of your reel. Lubrication of the reel becomes critical only when you are seeking distance casting. A simple way of keeping ordinary multipliers lubricated is to break them down and spray the works with something like WD-40, then just dab the spindles with a household oil like Three-in-One. Lubrication for distance casting I'll go into in the casting section that follows.

The fixed spool reel

Although gaining popularity as a shore reel, the fixed spool reel is still a long way from gaining widespread respectability among shore anglers. Like most sea anglers, I was educated to believe that the fixed spool reel was the domain of the novice and the part-timer and that proper sea anglers only used multipliers. A lot of sea anglers still believe that, but I don't any more. I use a fixed spool reel for cod fishing quite a lot.

Find yourself a typical bigoted multiplier man (yourself?) and ask why he wouldn't use a fixed spool reel for cod fishing. "Doesn't cast as far as a multiplier . . ." In terms of tournament distances this is true. But for the 99.9 per cent of sea anglers who've never seen, let alone taken part in, a tournament, there's every likelihood that they could cast further with a balanced fixed spool outfit than with their multiplier.

For the angler whose casting technique is less than perfect, there is always the threat of over-runs with a multiplier. Often one is afraid really to beef into the cast in case it costs you a trip to the tackle shop and a new spool of line. Of the few things you can't do with a fixed spool reel, getting an over-run is one of them. Because the lead only takes as much line as it wants by coiling off the lip of the spool, there can't be any over-runs. That means you can wrap the rod round your body and belt for all you're worth without a care in the world. If your cast is jerky, mis-timed, it won't matter. That is why I say a lot of anglers will cast further with a fixed spool outfit. There's even a bonus. Because you lose all fear of over-runs, you tend to develop a powerful style, which will get you increased distances when you turn back to a multiplier.

Other immediate advantages of the fixed spool are that there is no difference in casting at night or in daylight. There's no problem of when to thumb the spool to stop it paying out any more line—when the weight hits the water it will cease to take any more line. Casting very bulky baits or casting into a strong headwind can cause over-runs with a multiplier but never with the fixed spool.

However, casting with a fixed spool isn't completely snag-free: the fixed spool reel has three limitations. First, as a boat fishing reel it's a complete non-starter. The reason why the reel is unsuitable for fishing from a boat ties in to snag two; that of difficulty in reeling in a weight. Because of the way the fixed spool coils in the line, and the exceptionally high gear ratio some of them use, it is much more difficult to wind in the same weight with a fixed spool than with a conventional multiplier. You can get round this by pumping rather than directly reeling in all the time. Pumping is using the rod to lift the weight, then dropping the tip smartly and taking in the slack line. If you attempt to reel in a heavy weight on a fixed spool reel without pumping, you could damage the works through undue stress but will certainly restrict your next cast by having the line cut deeply into itself on the spool.

The final snag is that you can only use a fixed spool successfully with light lines. Ideally 12 lb., but no more than 18 lb. The reason the fixed spool reel will not allow you to cast as far as you would with a multiplier is because of the drag of the line coming over the lip of the spool. When the line begins to drop away from the lip of the spool there is a considerable amount of drag. So obviously, you have to limit this drag as much as possible. You do this by using line of as thin a diameter as possible (diameter being directly proportionate to the strength of the line).

You must also ensure that the spool is loaded to as near the lip of the spool as you dare have it. I cannot give you an exact distance as it varies from spool to spool, but it should be something around an eighth of an inch. If you attempt to load too much onto the spool it will fall off in great knotted coils that are the devil of a job to sort out. I was warned abut this when I first began using a fixed spool reel but dared to wind a little more on each time I renewed the line. Then came the day when I learned the hard way about overloading and I didn't do it again.

If you just wind line onto a fixed spool reel without any thought of how much the spool will take, you either end up with too much line and have to cut some away, or more likely not enough, leaving the line too far away from the lip of the spool. The capacity of large fixed spool reels is far in excess of what it needs to be. Those big, deep spools can take three or four hundred yards of line before they start to get full. Unless you particularly wish to fill the spool up with line, and there is no earthly reason for doing so, fill up the bottom half of the spool with a thick backing line. Ordinary string is as good as anything as it is thick, yet has a slight cushioning effect. I then cover all this backing with a few winds of vinyl insulation tape to prevent the actual fishing line from cutting into it.

Two hundred yards is as much line as most anglers need to put on the spool, though if you feel you are going to be banging out distances around the 150 yards plus mark, then make it 250 yards. It is very unlikely that you will have guessed the exact amount of backing and that the new line you wind on comes exactly to the lip. More likely it will be a bit short or a bit over. If there isn't enough line on, take some old thick line and wind that on top of the new line until it fills up the spool to the required depth. Then wind off that old line onto a spare spool, reel or with an old line holder, and then wind off all 200 yards of the new line and put the extra backing on top of the existing backing and tape over that.

Now rewind the new line onto the reel and it will fill exactly to the lip of the spool. I use spare fishing reels for this transferring of line. I also made some special wooden bobbins that fit into the bit of an electric drill, but even if you have to walk the line out round a field, do not be tempted to wind line off the spool by hand. You will kink it before you even begin to cast. To avoid kinking, you should also wind line from the plastic spool it comes on, not by putting a pencil through the middle and letting the spool revolve as you should with a multiplier, but by up-ending the spool and sitting it on the floor and letting the line coil off the end. The line comes off in hoops this way, but the bale arm picks up those hoops and lies them flat on the reel spool. It isn't an easy thing to explain in words, but watch carefully the next time you wind line onto a fixed spool reel and you will see what I mean.

Kinking is something you can't avoid with a fixed spool reel, and the end of the line usually comes from uncontrollable kinking rather than natural wear and tear. If you do lose some of the line, don't just carry on as normal, you will have to remove all of the line and increase the backing to compensate for the lost line so that the line does not fall away from the lip of the spool and restrict your casting. If this happens, I also reverse the line at the same time.

If your backing has been wound on level, you could well find that by the time you have finished filling up the reel with line there is a hump or a depression. It must be a common design fault that causes this, though it's easy to rectify. Make a mental note of how the lumps and bumps form on the reel and compensate for them when you wind on the backing, with a bit more in a spot where there is a depression and a bit less if there is a hump. This way you will end up with the line filled level on the reel. See Figure 4.

The choice of breaking strain I restrict to either my 12 lb. or 17 lb. breaking strain. I also use a line of less than normal diameter, but that is explained more fully in the section dealing with line. With these lines a leader is obviously needed. I use 50 lb. Three turns of leader on the spool is ample to withstand the shock of casting, but just before you cast, wind the leader round the spool by hand so that the leader knot is at the back of the spool and the three turns are in front of the knot. This way the line will not drag over the knot at the start of the cast.

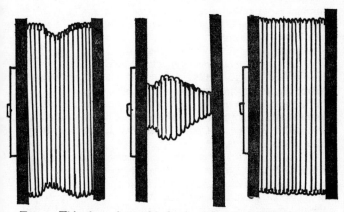

FIG. 4. This shows how with fixed spool reels the line does not wind on level, but creates humps and hollows. (a) shows the humps; (b) shows the correction made in the lay of the backing line, and (c) shows the finished effect after the line has been rewound back onto the reel – a level line.

Unless you have fingers of steel, some kind of protection for the release finger is needed. The choices are a glove, a finger stall or a Thumbutton. I don't think there's anything to choose between all three: it's a matter of personal choice. If you haven't used a Thumbutton I suggest you buy one and try it. They aren't everyone's favourite but are certainly worth trying. The beauty of a device like the Thumbutton release is that unlike a finger stall or a glove, you can't lose or forget it when you go fishing. I did that once and after a few casts my forefinger went raw. If you are unfamiliar with even what a Thumbutton looks like, it is a small button that is fixed to the butt and the line is trapped behind it by your thumb pressing on a button. When you lift your thumb off, the line is released. Quite ingenious really. If you buy a finger stall, get the suede or leather type, buy two and always keep a spare in your bag.

As cod fishing invariably involves chucking a long way on ground where you can use lines of 12 lb. and 17 lb. you need a model that will allow you to cast as far as possible, and that restricts the numbers to choose from. In a nutshell, you want the biggest reel you can get. With a large spool, at the end of the cast the line will still be fairly near the lip of the spool, so important for distance casting. If you use a smaller reel, 150 yards of line could be halfway down the spool, with a heck of a lot of drag to contend with.

For casting ability, the Mitchell 488 or 489 (left-hand and right-hand versions) is among the leaders. It is soundly constructed though cumbersome to use. I also have a Diawa Silver 7000C which is comfortable to use, casts very well, but unfortunately the material it is made from is poor. Twelve months after I got it the lip of the spool became pitted and I've had to replace it. I don't think that should happen to a 12 months' old reel.

I'll briefly mention here the importance of the right rod rings when using a fixed spool reel. Not only is there drag when you cast because of the line having to run over the lip of the spool, there is also drag as it chafes against the side of the rod rings. Also, the line comes from the reel in a wide coil. If it immediately meets a great number of narrow diameter rings—as you will find on most multiplier rods—you will have a considerable reduction in your cast. It could be as much as twenty to thirty yards. You must have a rod that is ringed specially for using a fixed spool reel. The theme of ringing for a fixed spool reel is large diameter and not many of them.

I particularly like the Fuji Braced Ceramic Sides rings. On my fixed spool rod I have three rings and a glue on tip ring. There are no rings on the butt section. The three rings are evenly spaced on the tip section and the three sizes I have are (inside diameters in millimetres) 40, 25, 16 and the tip is 16 mm. You can play around with the spacing and the sizes but I doubt that there will be much difference in your distances.

That, then, is the fixed spool reel. If you have never used one and you fish on ground where lines of the breaking strains I have suggested are used, then buy yourself one, ring a rod correctly and have a go. I doubt anyone will regret the buy, and many may wish they'd done it sooner.

The Scarborough reel

It will doubtless be a source of amusement to some that I should, in this day, discuss the Scarborough reel as a serious piece of angling equipment. To anyone unfamiliar with their use it must seem painfully old hat for anyone even to admit to owning one, let alone actually fishing with one. In the rougher parts of Yorkshire, Durham, Tyne and Wear, the Scarborough reel in skilled hands will yield more fish than any multiplier.

The reason is quite straightforward: the ground in this area is so rough that extremely heavy lines must be used to stand any chance of pulling through the rough. A breaking strain of between 50 and 60 lb. is about average. The stresses imposed on a reel when you are winding in with that kind of pressure are more than the multiplier is made to stand. Physically, it becomes near impossible to wind in with a high gear ratio, yet you want that high recovery rate to get the tackle or fish moving up off the bottom as soon as possible.

A good eight-inch Scarborough reel will withstand any kind of pressure. The bursting of side plates on Scarboroughs is very rare. The ratio is 1 : 1 so you can keep on winding with a Scarborough when you would be forced to stop with a multiplier. The recovery rate of a Scarborough is good by virtue of the very deep drum. The advantages should now become clear.

When I talk about the rough ground of the North East as being special, I mean that it presents very great physical obstacles. We all have our own ideas of what is a rough beach, but you cannot compare your own rough patch until you have fished in the North East.

There must be a biological reason why so much kelp grows in the North Sea from Flamborough Head to the Scottish Border, but perhaps the great number of boulders and rocks plays a part. The two together certainly present the cod angler with the roughest ground in England or Scotland.

27

I have seen competent anglers simply shake their heads after looking at the ground at places like Whitley Bay, Tynemouth, Scarborough and Flamborough. At low water all the eye can see is a brown, waving mass of solid weed. There might be a few square yards of clear sea and that is where you aim to cast. I do sometimes wonder how the bait ever manages to reach the bottom with so much dense weed. Casting through the hole will enable you to reach the bottom, but the moment you commence reeling in, you have to drag right through those clawing tentacles of weed. Tyneside in the rough was described once as being like the dark side of the moon—with kelp—and I can't better that description.

There are clear spots where the multiplier can be used with ease of mind, but when you head for the heavy ground you use multipliers at the risk of seeing them disintegrate.

With so many hazards in the water, casting any kind of a distance is more a hindrance than a help. The further out you are, the more obstacles you have to pass to get your tackle in. Apart from which, the cod tend to come in close to the rock edges where the weed abounds, so a cast of over 40 yards isn't necessary.

Until you have fished in this highly physical way, with arms aching from the stress of pulling a fish through this heavy ground, you cannot judge whether this style is crude, antiquated or very pleasurable. But I don't know any of the North East's most successful anglers who don't bow to the superiority of this reel on the really hard ground.

One problem that all acknowledge is the difficulty in buying a really good Scarborough reel. Walk into any good tackle shop in the North East and you will see on display a whole range of Scarborough reels, from small three-inch models up to ten-inch reels, for boat angling. But for cod fishing from the shore, the king of them all is the oil-bath Scarborough. This is a reel that has a centre spindle constructed of two cones with the drum revolving on these cones and the whole works swimming in a medium viscosity grease.

The cones are adjustable, as with bicycle wheel cones, so that free play can be kept to a minimum, and the grease not only allows the drum to spin very freely, but prevents corrosion. With so few moving parts the life-span of the oil-bath reel is limitless, which may have a bearing on why they are only manufactured in small quantities.

I've written this section on the Scarborough reel not to try to convert anyone; I know that their application applies only to the North East of England where all know their worth already. It's been included because I want to try to eradicate some of the misconceptions about this reel. So that those who have no use for it will not pour scorn on those who have. And for those still unconvinced, just pop along to the next Tynemouth Open and try to fish St Mary's Island with normal tackle. Four hours there and cod fishing will never quite be the same again for you.

Lines

Nylon monofilament is the only line that most cod anglers will ever use. A few may use already—or might try after reading this book—braided fabric lines for certain types of fishing, but for most, mono is the only one.

All line begins life as a pot of molten nylon. The chemical formula does vary slightly from manufacturer to manufacturer, but basically all mono line is the same stuff. In this initial stage the nylon is a pale translucent substance. The host of different colours that you can get line in are determined at this stage by nothing more complicated than dye. You can go into a well-stocked tackle shop and buy line of any colour, so the next time someone tries to tell you that brown Bloggs line is better than blue Bloggs line tell 'em the truth.

There are very few manufacturers in Western Europe that make mono fishing line. It is a very competitive business without much profit (so one manufacturer told me). A great many of the dozens of different brands you see in the shops are, in fact, the same line, just on a different label. If you order enough from a manufacturer he'll dye it a special colour for you, possibly marginally alter the formula and draw it to the diameters you want. But if I wanted to market Bob Gledhill Brand fishing line, all I would have to do would be to design my own label and the rest would be done for me. This is how some of the larger tackle dealers get their own brand line.

It isn't necessary to understand the chemistry of fishing line to be able to tell good from bad, but I'll explain very simply how line is made and why the prices of different brands vary and why they perform differently.

It starts out as small granules of solid nylon, or polymer as it is called. The manufacturer heats it to a liquid and draws it out through a die. As it is being drawn, it is also passed through a series of rollers, with one pair of rollers travelling faster than the set behind it, thus creating tension in the line and altering the molecular structure. It is also given heat by infra-red heaters which add to the tempering of the line.

The more the molecules in the line are brought into alignment with each other, the stronger the line becomes for a given diameter, but this also increases the brittleness. This is the principal of the very low-stretch lines and explains why you get sudden breaks with these premium lines.

Elongation is the amount a line will stretch before breaking and can be expressed as a percentage. Elongation is governed by the alignment of the molecules. A line that is produced from short-length molecules, and not rolled to a high ratio will be very stetchy with an elongation factor of up to 45 per cent. Premium, low-stretch lines may have an elongation factor as low as 15 per cent, though most lines fall between 25 to 35 per cent. Elongation becomes important in distance fishing when a stretchy line will be difficult to set a hook with.

Creep in a line is also important. When you tension a line to breaking point (e.g. when you get fastened up round a snag), and then release the line, you want the line to return to its original shape (or as near as possible). If it loses diameter it will also lose strength. The loss factor is called creep and if you have a line where the creep is high, it will quickly become useless.

The piece of line that receives the most tension is the last few yards that takes the impact of the cast. No line can stand a day's continual casting without creeping considerably and losing strength. That is why it is best to discard the last few yards of line before each session or tie on a new leader.

Nylon is affected by the ultra-violet light from the sun. The ultra-violet rays cause a weak spot in the molecular chain so when a tensioning of the line occurs, it will part at the point where the line has been weakened. But for ultra-violet to cause perceptible damage to the line it would have to be exposed for weeks on end, and of course line isn't. You are far more likely to damage the line by a sharp stone than by ultra-violet light from the sun.

Nylon is hygroscopic (it absorbs water). What happens is that water molecules get between the nylon molecules and expand the line slightly and weaken it. There is a fairly rapid loss as soon as the line is wet, but total saturation takes a long time. The maximum break load loss you could expect is ten per cent. When the line dries out it returns to normal.

So the difference in price of line comes from the quality of the raw nylon and the amount of processing it goes through in manufacture to correct the natural flaws in nylon.

The most unreliable aspect of buying line is the breaking strain according to the label. A manufacturer can keep the diameter fairly consistent, but not the strength. I could walk into any tackle shop armed with a spring balance and have trouble finding a line that broke at the strength claimed for it.

Take a length of 20 lb. line. When you first tie a knot in it, it can lose at least ten per cent in strength. You cast it out and the end section is strained and might suffer a further ten per cent loss by the end of the day. You get fastened up round a rock but fortunately manage to pull out, but not before a ten per cent loss of strength. At the end of the day, just for curiosity, we test the line round a spring balance. What does our 20 lb. line register? Just 14½ lb. We complain bitterly next day in the tackle shop.

That was an imaginary case, but you can do a much more positive test of accuracy. Get a spring balance and ask your dealer for a foot length of line from a spool of 18 lb. line. Put a loop in either end and hook one loop round a pencil and the other round the spring balance, and pull. I did this with a tackle dealer one quiet afternoon and we did it with the cheapest and the best, and the results went from 13 lb. to 16 lb. for all but one line. And that one broke at 19 lb.! Surprisingly, on none of the test lengths did the line break at the knot. If they had have done, then we would have allowed for some loss of strength. But as all broke in the middle, I don't feel we have to give any tolerance.

I once bought a 500 yard spool of 35 lb. line from a major British retailer, and sent it back without taking it off the spool because it smashed at 28 lb. on my spring balance. The retailer simply sent it back with the curt reply that line *never* broke at the strength claimed.

If someone had a mind to, they could cause all sorts of problems for the retail trade by complaining that the line is not as described on the label—illegal under The Sale of Goods Act 1893 as amended by The Supply of Goods (Implied Terms) Act 1973. I think the day will soon come when labels will carry either no stated strength at all, or modify the strength as 'approx so many pounds, when dry and un-knotted'.

Which breaking strains to use depends on the type of terrain you are fishing, and the distance you wish to cast. Thinner lines cast further than thicker ones—thicker ones don't break as easy as thin ones. If you want to cast a long way and the ground is clear, drop down to 12 lb. If there are a few small snags—perhaps some weed, but you still want to bang it out, try 18 lb. For quite rough ground with fair amounts of weed and stone, use 25 lb. to 35 lb. according to how rough it is. For dense kelp and boulders use 50 lb.

Those figures are certainly not fixed—you can juggle with them to suit yourself. If you are losing too much gear, then step up the line, if you aren't casting far enough and there are few snags, drop it down. Everyone will need a shock leader for lines under 25 lb., some may need one for up to 35 lb. Play it by ear.

Two exceptions to this reckoning are fishing when there is a lot of loose, floating weed and fishing in very fast currents such as estuaries. When there is that clinging, loose weed about, it gathers on your line like washing, slipping down until it finally jams at the leader knot. With lines less than 18 lb., the pull of the surf on this great mass of weed could smash you, and certainly you will never get the leader knot through the top ring. Cleaning the weed off the line is the devil of a job and makes fishing very unpleasant.

For this reason I do not use a leader when fishing in these conditions. With a level line of 28 lb., the weed will stop very near the end of the line, possibly around a swivel or a bait, and to clear it all off, the simplest way is to cut the line, slide all the weed off, then knot the line again.

The other exception to this scale of line strengths is when fishing in a tide race. The biggest problem in fishing these places is preventing the tide from sweeping your tackle down tide and into the shore. The usual way of preventing this is to put heavy line and an anchor lead on, hoping that the anchor will dig in and hold. By all means use an anchor, but instead of increasing the line diameter, reduce it. The surface area of the line is what the tide drags, not the terminal tackle. If the surface area of 100 yards of 30 lb. were to be converted into a more recognisable shape, it would be a sheet of plastic, something like nine inches by nine inches. No wonder it would need so much lead to hold it in position. Reduce the diameter of the line, and consequently the surface area of resistance, then you won't need as much lead and it will hold fast much easier.

The choice from the three varieties of line is not only which is best suited for the job, but which is the most economic in use. If you have heavy losses you just can't afford to keep paying out several pounds a week on line. My yardstick is to use cheap bulk line on 35 lb. and over, and a pre-stretched line for the weaker strengths. There are several excellent makes, but the one I have stuck with for a while now is the Nylorfi brand, distributed by Farlow's. The heavy bulk spool line I buy is Sylcast.

For general boat fishing, I use 18 lb. line. I've landed plenty of cod heavier than 18 lb. on 18 lb. line, and have yet to be broken by a cod. If I am fishing for really heavy cod or on rough ground, or if the boat is drifting, then I use something in the order of 28 lb. For normal cod fishing nothing heavier than that is necessary.

The cod fishing off my bit of coastline is in shallow water and the fish don't run very big. Coupled to that, the bottom is shingly sand or mud, so there are few obstacles. For this reason I frequently use 12 lb. line and it has yet to be broken by a cod. There is no logical reason for using line heavier than 30 lb. for cod fishing unless conditions are very special.

Few anglers ever apply more than 20 lb. of pressure at the rod tip, and you can prove it very easily. Set a boat rod up with just a big hook on the end. Loop this under a bucket handle, load 20 lb. of lead into the bucket and try to lift it. It'll feel as if you're trying to lift 40 lb., and the tip will be at a ninety degree arc. Remember how hard it is to reel a cod of just a few pounds up the side of a pier. That is invoking the same law of levers that makes it difficult to lift the weighted bucket.

And of course the lighter the line, the less its diameter and thus the less lead you will need.

But having argued that point, I'll admit to using 40 lb. braided terylene for pirk fishing. Braided lines are a must for deep water pirking—which much of mine is—for reasons I'll explain in the section on lure fishing. The reason for such a heavy line, however, is purely enconomic. Even though I make many of my own lures, they are still too valuable to lose on the bottom. As the very nature of pirk fishing demands that it

C.F.—B

is worked along the bottom, lures are very prone to getting caught up on obstructions. You lose fewer lures with 40 lb. line than with 20 lb. It's as simple as that.

Hooks

To write about the different types of hooks for catching cod it is necessary to consider the different styles of cod fishing and the hook best suited to it. Firstly, there are a lot of inferior hooks on the market. Hooks that snap, straighten or are shaped wrongly. Bluntness can be expected with all hooks, but that is easily corrected. What cannot be forgiven is the hook which snaps or straightens while a cod is on, resulting in the loss of the fish.

Snapping is the worst sin of all for a hook, because even if the hook straightens slightly there is still a chance that the barb will hold. If the hook snaps, however, it's all over. I've been told that the safest way to buy hooks is to test one from a box of a hundred and if that is good, the rest will be. I disagree. You can get a mixture of qualities in a box. Soft ones, brittle ones and just right ones. The only safe way to find good hooks is to test each one individually. My test is quite simple—I try to straighten it with my fingers. If I can't straighten it, I know no cod will. I also check that the barb has not been cut too deeply, so weakening the hook point, and that it is not standing out too far.

I only use two types of hooks for cod fishing: fine wire and bronze forged. The fine wire hooks I buy are either Cannelle or Edgar Sealey. In the smaller sizes the Mustad hook is soft and I do not recommend it. In bronze forged I use Edgar Sealey Flashpoint—when I can get hold of them—(supplies seem limited), or Sundridge Specimen Long Shank (check these carefully for brittleness), or the Mustad 79510, which is a fine wire bronze forged hook. There are a few more good bronze forged hooks on sale, but whichever you choose, beware of thick wire and too big a barb. Stainless steel hooks are strong but difficult to keep sharp. I have used beaked hooks and found no advantage in them.

The smallest hook size I use for cod is a 1/0. I go as small as that if I'm on a beach where the cod never run very big and where there is the chance of a few whiting as well. The size I use mostly is a 3/0 which is capable of handling a big cod over fairly rough ground but is not so thick in the wire or barb as to hinder striking.

If I'm on rough ground and expecting hefty fish I'll go up to 5/o, but bigger than that—9/o—I only use when I'm in a boat and expect very heavy fish and am using very big baits. Remember that the measurements of hooks as expressed by the /o scale varies considerably from manufacturer to manufacturer. Another good guide to which size to use is the size of the bait. As a rule of thumb, use big hooks for big baits, so the bait doesn't unduly mask the hook point and impede it setting.

A further factor that influences the choice of hook pattern and size is the distance at which you are fishing. Fishing at great range means that a lot of the impact of the strike is absorbed by the stretch in the line, so if you have a thick wire and large barb it will not penetrate the flesh of a cod's mouth as easily as a fine wire hook with a small barb.

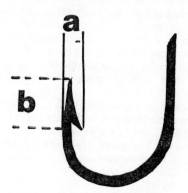

FIG. 5. Anatomy of a hook point.

Figure 5 illustrates this point. The two measurements arrowed govern the penetrating power of the hook. Distance (b) is how deep inside the flesh the hook has to go before the barb holds on. Distance (a) is the width of the hole the hook has to make in the flesh before the hook can set. The ease with which the hook can slide through the flesh past the barb is also governed by the thickness of the wire from the outer tip of the barb to the hook point.

35

You will obviously notice that there is a considerable difference in distance (a) and distance (b) on 2/o hook compared with a 5/o hook. For this reason a smaller hook will set easier at distance than a larger hook.

There is probably as much cod fishing carried on over rough ground as there is over clean ground, and in rough ground fishing you need a different set of qualities for your hook. Obviously you still need penetrating power, but that can become secondary to holding power. Once you have got the fish on, the hook must not straighten or snap under pressure.

Fishing over rough ground goes hand in hand with heavier lines, which in turn allow greater stress to be applied to the hook. With lines of 30 lb. and over (and I've explained in the Line section why they *are* necessary), fine wire hooks are likely to be the weakest point in your tackle. The problem arises when a fish—it may only be a few pounds—takes a quick turn round a lump of weed or rock, and the line gets jammed. You have to literally skull-drag the fish through the obstacle and a fine wire hook might not take that kind of pressure, so on heavy ground with heavy tackle, use forged hooks in a large size to withstand the strain. The hooking power may not be as good as that of a smaller hook, but you are invariably fishing at a closer range on this sort of ground, so there is a compensation factor there for the thicker hook.

I believe in sharpening hooks. I used to think that sharpening hooks was something that freshwater anglers did, and like many sea anglers, I just took a hook from the box without any thought whatever. The number of bites I have successfully connected with has increased considerably since I began to care for my hooks. That isn't an idle statement, but something I sincerely believe is true.

The first problem I came to when I decided I would begin sharpening hooks, was with what, and how. The first thing I bought was a stone that claimed to be a hook sharpener. The stone was too rough and it didn't make the hooks any sharper than when I started. I progressed to a small oilstone, but the problem with that was working inside the bend of the hook. Next came a small flat watchmaker's file. That was too rough for small hooks but is perfect for hooks over 6/o.

The solution came quite by chance. I had discovered that the small watchmaker's file was the right shape for covering all the angles on a hook, but that the cut of the file was too coarse. I was explaining to an ironmonger the type of file I wanted when he suddenly produced a box of emery boards, the things women use to shape and sharpen their nails. I took one home and tried it. The grit came away easily from the soft card backing but it worked reasonably well. I wanted a grit that would cut through metal instead of female talons, and the obvious answer was fine emery paper, and on a firm backing.

I cut a thin strip of plywood, 8 cm. by 1 cm., coated it in Evo-Stick and wrapped the fine grade emery paper round it. To get perfect adhesion I then clamped it up in a vice for a second or two. I trimmed round the board with a pair of scissors and in a couple of minutes had created my ideal hook sharpener. The emery tends to dull after a short while so they are not long-lasting, but they are so quick to make that you can throw them away every couple of weeks.

Having created my hook sharpener, the next step was to determine the best method of using it and the correct angle. If you take off too much, the hook point will be needle-sharp but so fragile it will bend over at the slightest bump and be blunter than when you started. Too flat, and again you are worse off than when you started. Figure 6 shows the angle I aim for in sharpening hooks. (a) is too severe, (b) not severe enough, and (c) is just right.

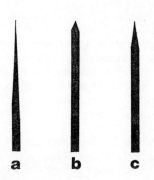

a   b   c

Fig. 6. The right and wrong shapes of hook points.

There are two ways of doing the sharpening: the all-round cut and the wedge cut. The all-round cut is done by holding the hook with the point facing upwards and stroking the sharpener in an upwards direction at the approximate angle shown in Figure 6 (c). To ensure that the hook is equally ground on all sides, I think of the hook as being square, giving an equal number of strokes on four sides. Do not rock the sharpener when using it, or else you will get a curved point. To test if the hook is sufficiently sharp, slowly pull the point over the back of your hand. It should dig in. Pricking the point with a fingertip isn't recommended as the tips of fingers can become quite insensitive through certain use.

The wedge cut I do on two opposing sides using either an emery sharpener or a smooth watchmaker's file, and this is useful on hooks above 5/o. Instead of holding the hook by hand while you are sharpening it, these larger sizes can either be clamped in a small vice or you can lay the hook flat on its side on top of the file and draw it up over the cutting teeth. This ensures you get a flat surface on the hook.

You can see the lack of sharpness on a hook point by putting it under a microscope. I went into the science lab. at my local tech. and put a variety of hooks under the microscope. On hooks around 9/o there was a flat surface that two fleas could have had a game of football on, and even on 1/o hooks they looked terribly blunt. I sharpened some of the hooks there and then and looked again, and there was a much greater improvement, though I still couldn't get a needle point on very large hooks.

If you look back to Figure 5, that distance B from the outer tip of the barb to the shank is much more than it needs to be. Obviously with a tighter barb, penetration will be easier, so I close up slightly all the barbs on my hooks using a pair of pliers. If you are dubious about the holding power of a reduced barb, just have a dry run with one the next time you get a cod. Pull the hook into the cod's mouth as you would with a normal strike, then try to shake it out. You won't succeed.

For tying hooks to line, I use nothing but a half blood knot, but with an extra tuck. The extra tuck comes at the end of the knot when the line is passed through the bottom loop next to the hook eye. After you have pushed the line through this bottom loop, bring it round and push it through again—then pull tight after wetting the knot. The extra tuck will bite into the knot and stop the knot from just pulling out, something that happens with thick line and large hooks. See Figure 7.

38

Finally, on keeping hooks after they have been sharpened up, I dip them in fish oil, wipe them off then tape them between two strips of Sellotape in strips of five or six. This protects the points, stops them rusting and allows you to do an important chore in the comfort of an armchair.

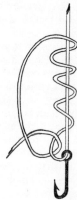

FIG. 7. The tucked half blood knot.

Terminal tackle

Before I get too deeply into how to tie a hook on, I'll discuss the number of hooks: one, two or three. It is reasonable to suppose that with three hooks you stand more chance of catching cod from the shore. You can present three different baits or three of the same kind and increase the scent three-fold. You may also catch more than one cod at once. Should one bait fly off, be eaten by pests or a cod that got away, there is still bait left. So why is the one-hook rig so popular?

On shallow, clear beaches you often have to cast a long way to reach the fish. On rocky, weedy beaches you don't have to cast as far but there are hundreds of potential snags between your bait and the shore, and the more hooks, the more chances of getting fastened up.

That should answer the question of why the one-hook rig is so popular. More than one hook is a two-time loser on most beaches. Where there are no snags, if you were to use three hooks you would suffer a dramatic fall in your casting range and lose fish that way. If you were to use a multiple hook trace on a snaggy beach where distance was not so important, you might lose fish through getting the other hooks fastened up round snags while trying to bring a fish in.

There is an in-between zone where multiple-hook rigs have few snags, but I've yet to be convinced that in cod fishing they bring much greater success than would a single-hook rig. So the discussion that follows will concern single-hook rigs.

I was talking to a young angler recently and he asked me a very basic, simple question. He wanted to know how long a snood should be when he was cod fishing from the shore. It probably seemed a very straightforward question to him, but it took me so long to answer that by the time I'd finished I'm sure he was more puzzled than before I began.

A snood in my vocabulary is the hook-length—the piece of line that fastens the hook to the main line.

I think snood lengths in sea fishing are a bit like shotting patterns in floatfishing in that two anglers seldom agree for long. It isn't hard to figure out which is the best snood length if you tend to stay round your own patch all the time—the best length is probably going to be the one that everyone else uses, because it's tried and tested on your beach. But if you begin travelling for your cod fishing up and down the country, the variations on the theme of a hook snood become mind-bending.

I've seen (and used) snoods of 5 ft.–6 ft. and as short as 6 in., though most anglers seem to go for something around 18 in. The obvious answer as to which is best is to see which is the most effective in terms of cod caught. But it isn't as simple as that. Anglers take good catches of cod on snoods at either end of the length scale, so how do you tell the user of one extreme that he'd catch any different with 5 ft. more (or less) of snood?

The shortest snoods I've ever seen in popular use are those used by the locals in the Isle of Man. There 6 in. is about standard. When I asked a Manx friend why he used such a short snood length, he reckoned the shorter snood lengths led to better bite detection and with a short snood he could hook the fish quicker. But his main reason for using a short snood was because he caught more fish with one that length. And you don't get a better reason than that.

As we weren't fishing for anything more than fun at the

time, I tied up a very short snood and found that it didn't make any difference to the number of fish we were catching. I then swopped to a five-footer (much to the horror of my friend) and guess what? No difference again.

The longest snoods I've seen anyone use regularly are the 5 ft.–6ft. lengths popular in Whitley Bay and Tynemouth. Over twelve months this area probably produces more cod than anywhere in Britain, so the Whitley lads have more chances than anybody to learn the right snood lengths. They argue that the longer lengths give the cod more time to take the bait and allow it to ride more naturally in the water. Whether you agree with their reasoning or not, what you cannot escape from is their success rate with snoods of this length. They use them not only in their native Geordieland but also in the West of Scotland and they wallop fish out with no problem using these long snoods. Just in case you think the type of ground holds the key to which snoods fish the best, let me repeat that I've seen long and short used side by side without any apparent difference.

The answer to the question *how long* is that if you have got everything else right about your tackle, bait and choice of spot, it doesn't really matter how long your snood is—you'll still take fish. But I believe that by changing the length of your snood you can, in some cases, catch more.

The first rule of snood length is that the length has no bearing on the amount of bites you get. It does, however, have an effect on the number of those bites you connect with. The time between the fish taking the bait and signalling the take either through the line or via the rod, is governed on most occasions by the length of the snood.

I think it is reasonable to suppose that when a cod takes a baited hook and feels the resistance of the weight, the rod tip, or feels the hook point prick its mouth, it will spit the bait out. (Of course there are exceptions, but in order to make my point I'll discount them). To go to a complete extreme, if I used a 3 in. snood, the cod would only have to move its head slightly with the bait in its mouth for it to feel the resistance and signal the bite. The fish lets go and all you have had is a short, sharp pull. It can take lightning reflexes to connect cod bites like those.

At the other end of the scale, imagine a 12 ft. snood. The fish picks the bait up and it may have to move the bait a couple of feet before any resistance (and thus the bite) is felt. In that time the cod could have taken the bait well down and be firmly hooked before you even see the bite. The bite you get from a very long snood tends to be a longer and firmer pull than with a very short snood. The cod seems to give a few moments longer to hit the bite with long snoods. But there is the obvious problem with an extremely long snood of not being able to cast it, which is why 6 ft. is the upper practical limit.

There is another disadvantage to the long snood and that is when the cod are not making searing runs but just chomping away on the spot. With a long snood you might never see bites like that.

I've magnified both extremes to illustrate the principle more clearly, but the best way of showing yourself how bites are registered is to do a mock-up in the back garden. Tie up a set of terminal gear and spread it out on the ground. Tighten up the line in the normal way and the first thing you will see is that the snood lies alongside the main line. This contradicts the way traces are often illustrated as lying at a nice untangled forty-five degree angle to the main line.

Then simply start taking the hook like a fish would—which is all sorts of ways. Give a gentle backward pull, a hard yank, sideways, forwards. Try it with different snood lengths. The reaction on the rod tip will be grossly distorted at such a short range, but it gives you an idea of how different snood lengths react in the water. Watch particularly for the time from when the hook is picked up to when it meets the resistance of the line and the bite is registered. This will show clearly the point of short snoods and quicker bites, long snoods and longer bites.

In Figure 8 you will see the three basic shapes that a one-hook trace can be. You can experiment with different lengths for both the weight length and the snood and you will get varying reactions. Notice how the direction in which the fish takes the bait can be an influencing factor in the time lapse between take and bite being signalled.

Now comes the tricky bit. When to use a long one and when to use a short one. Remember I said earlier that I don't believe it makes a great deal of difference, but if you find you are missing a lot of bites (possibly from smaller fish), shorten your snood length and be prepared to hit the bites very quickly. If you are missing bites and you think they are from good fish, try a longer snood to give the cod more time with the bait. If you are getting just one bite, then the cod are not coming back, try a longer snood, again to give the cod more time with the bait. But as a general all-round length, 18 in. to 2 ft. will succeed on any beach I've ever fished.

Having thought about the length of the hook snood, there is now the problem of attaching it to the main line. It is a problem because all snoods tend to twist round and round the main line, effectively reducing the snood length to a couple of inches.

I have battled for years to eliminate this problem without much success. I've tried swivels, lines of different strengths, fancy knots, and the only things that have worked efficiently are small, home-made French booms just an inch long. But

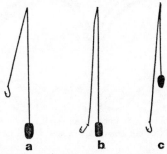

FIG. 8. The three basic designs of a single-hook trace.

these are cumbersome things, they cut down the casting range, and I only use them with a fixed spool reel where there is a much greater tendency for the snood to spin round the main line. I make the little booms from fine stainless steel wire and the boom part is usually about 1 in.–2 in.

Another idea to reduce the effect of this spinning is to adopt a rig as in Figure 8 (c) where the snood hangs well below the weight. It doesn't matter how much spinning the snood does—it cannot tangle round anything. The use of a three-way swivel for making up a one-hook trace seems widespread, with the third eye of the swivel used for fastening the snood to in the belief that the swivel will stop tangling. It doesn't work. I don't think you get any less tangling with a three-way swivel than with just a plain knot.

The knotting system I use is to tie a blood loop in the weight line at the point to which I wish the snood to be joined. I tie an overhand loop in the end of the snood line and fasten the two loops together by passing the hook first through the main line loop, then through the loop on the end of the snood and pulling tight. I do not recommend you to use a half blood knot to fasten the snood to the loop on the main line. The snood pulling against the main line loop will have a cutting action and will create a weak point in your tackle. The blood loop knot and overhand loop knot are shown in Figures 9 and 10. In using any kind of knot be prepared for a strength loss of about 20 per cent in the breaking strength of the line.

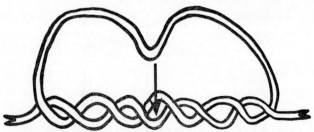

FIG. 9. The blood loop knot. After the line is passed through the coils where arrowed, the knot is pulled tight.

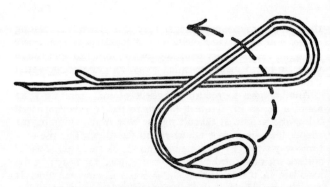

FIG. 10. The overhand loop knot. For extra security the loop can be passed through a second time.

The choice of weight for shore fishing depends on what suits your casting ability. A four, five and six ounce lead are all capable of being thrown a long way, though many anglers find difficulty with a six ounce lead when using a powerful casting style. The simplest way to find out which weight suits your casting technique is to go on a field and try all three. Then see which you feel most comfortable with and which casts the furthest.

The speed of the tide isn't a major influence on what weight of lead to choose. You will overcome tackle drift much more easily by reducing your line diameter than by increasing your weight. Anyway, if your favourite casting weight doesn't hold firm, use an anchor lead. By keeping to the same weight whenever possible you become familiar with how much power to apply and at which point in your casting.

I don't think the shape of the weight has much importance as long as it is streamlined to reduce air-resistance. I do not like round torpedo shapes as they have a tendency to roll on the bottom and cause line twist. The shape I use is called Aquapedo, a four flat-sided lead.

Drifting of the tackle is not caused by the tide pushing the lead along the bottom but by the tide dragging on the line, causing a bow, and as the weight is dragged along, if it is circular it will twist, while the flat-sided leads will tend to keep the same position as they drift.

The only shape that is drag-resistant (other than a wired anchor) is the pyramid shape. It's only a guess, but I think the tide rises up over the pyramid then presses it down.

For boat fishing I have a bell-shaped mould which can produce leads up to 2 lb. Score a line on the inside of your mould at predetermined weights, i.e. a line at 6 oz., 12 oz., 1 lb., 1½ lb.

Shop-bought lead weights are so expensive that it's small wonder many anglers now cast their own. There is no shortage of firms advertising in the angling press with various moulds for sale, and whichever shape you opt for, the only advice I would give is to have it drilled for anchor wires so that you can make both ordinary and anchor leads with it.

What I would strongly advise is that you treat molten lead with great respect. Everything you use in melting down lead must be absolutely dry. Even a drop of water in a pot of molten lead will cause violent spitting, possibly an explosion. If you are melting down anything that is suspect, particularly old lead piping, dry it out in front of the fire first, and don't stand over it while it melts down. A pair of asbestos gloves from an army and navy stores will allow you to handle moulds and ladle while they are hot.

You can make the loops by stripping down scrap heavy duty electrical cable for the copper wire, but let them sink into the body of the weight for at least an inch so that they don't pull out during casting.

For anchor wires, keep your eyes open for brass wire, stainless steel wire, even the welding rods that are used in acetylene welding. The longer the wires, the firmer they will grip. There is a problem here, however, and it comes from using light lines and anchor leads. The lead can be so firmly lodged in, that the strength needed to dislodge it is more than the line will stand. This is one of the ideas behind the Breakaway type of lead where the wires are hinged and locked into the body of the weight with beads in a recess. It takes more pressure than the tide can exert to pull the wires free, but less than the breaking point of the line.

Clothing

Oddly enough, clothing *can* contribute to the number of cod you catch. If you are wet and cold and the weather is biting through you, it's hard, near impossible to have the same amount of concentration in your fishing. If you are warm and dry, your mind can concentrate more on the job in hand.

As cod fishing is largely involved with winter and rough seas, a warm and dry outfit is a must. At one time I used to buy my fishing clothes from ex-army stores, or use old worn-out cast-offs, but not any more. I reasoned that while I was quite willing to spend £50 on a reel, it was silly to object to paying more than a few quid on clothing. So for the price of a new reel, I kitted out in the best weather gear I could buy— and have never regretted it. For winter fishing I have a head-to-foot outfit of Damart Double Force underwear. That is: socks, long johns, long-sleeved vest, balaclava and gloves. On top of that I have ordinary warm clothing and for the outer skin an all-in-one insulated weatherproof suit. This outfit keeps me warm and dry in boats and on the shore and is one of the best buys I ever made.

I'm not saying I keep warm all the time, but I can stand conditions that send others chattering to the car.

CHAPTER TWO

Baits

While I intend to go into great depth on how to get and keep all the popular cod baits, I can't tell you which is best, because the best bait differs from area to area. You have to find the best for yourself, all I can do is advise on getting and using.

In general, don't accept the myth that cod will eat anything. Just because plastic cups, bottle corks and the like are occasionally found in the stomachs of cod, don't believe that cod motor along the sea bed like vacuum cleaners, taking all in their paths. They can be very finicky, and are particularly prone to becoming preoccupied with one source of food, if it is plentiful.

Since I regard bait as one of the big three laws of cod catching (the right time and the right place are the other two), I never compromise on bait. I'll shiver and sweat to get what I want and frequently spend more time getting bait than actually fishing.

If you can't get down to the beach to get your own bait and have to rely on a bought supply, I recommend you to fix up a private deal with a professional supplier rather than rely on your local tackle shop having something. I know several groups of anglers who live well inland and operate a scheme like this for themselves, and they are never without good bait.

The way to go about it is to go to a beach where you know there are plenty of worms to be dug and ask around at low water, looking for those diggers with the brimming buckets. You'll have to be polite and discreet and convince the digger you aren't from the Inland Revenue, but it shouldn't be too difficult to find a digger prepared to supply you on a regular basis.

You may be expected to pay more to the digger than he gets from the shop, but even if you pay normal retail price, at least you will know the supply is regular and good. It will also involve you picking the worms up rather than having them delivered, and you must certainly never back off on an order.

If you live so far from the sea that even picking them up is impractical, then watch the classified columns of the angling press and pick yourself a wholesale supplier from there. You will have to pay for carriage charges, but again the supply should be reliable.

Just how important is fresh bait? Not such a straight-forward question. There are competent anglers who argue that lug that have blown to jelly can be as good, if not better, than fresh lug. And, of course, these people produce catches to back up their beliefs. Smell plays an important part in attracting a fish, and what is smellier than lug that have gone off? Who is to say that cod will not eat dead lugworms?

If you leave lug exposed to the air, bacteria begin to decompose the flesh and make it stink. We know that that smell is from decaying flesh, but does a fish? The bacteria that are causing the smell may be alien to a fish, so though the bait smells different, a fish might not associate it with something not to be eaten. Human beings often assume that fish react in a similar way to themselves. For example: I can find hardly any smell in a fresh-dug lugworm. Can I therefore assume that lugworm have no smell? Of course I can't, because I haven't the nose of a fish.

Some years ago I was a member of the Freshwater Bio-logical Association and visited the laboratory on Windermere. I was delving into the business of smell and one of the research students showed me an experiment with perch in a glass tank. He put a hypodermic into a lobworm and extracted a small amount of liquid from the worm. In a glass tank about two feet square was a perch of a few inches. The fish was lying fairly still at the bottom of the tank.

The hypodermic was held over the top of the tank and just the tiniest drop of that liquid was splashed onto the surface of the water. It was a colourless liquid, but we could see a greasy patch and it slowly began to descend. In seconds the perch became very agitated, swimming round the tank obviously hunting for the source of that smell. It continued its search for ten minutes before settling back. The particle we released into that water was so miniscule one would have thought it could have fallen righ past the perch and it would not have flinched. But we did not reckon on either the pungency of a worm, the powerful nose of the fish, or both.

I have no reason to doubt that something similar would

have happened had we done the experiment with a cod and lugworm.

I am not advocating the use of rotten lug for catching cod, but fresh lug is not the only thing to use. This business of smell is very complicated, a fundamental of all forms of sport fishing, yet something we don't know a great deal about.

A final point on smell, and that is not to let your bait lose too much of it by being washed out. The perch experiment shows that there is a great store of smell even in the smallest of baits but it is logical that the ability of a bait to attract from a distance is reduced if the bait has been left in the water a long time and become washed out.

To this end I always fish with a watch, and reel in and rebait to a time schedule. Fifteen minutes per bait is a good starting point, but this may have to be reduced if pests are taking the bait, or extended if you haven't a great deal of bait. Either way, I invariably change the bait completely at every cast.

A further advantage of this fishing by clock is that you can work out in advance approximately how much bait you are going to need per hour. When you work it out like that it's surprising how little bait you actually need for a fishing session. However, onto the baits themselves.

Peeler Crab

The study of shore crabs—when and where they peel—has been a side-hobby of mine for a number of years. Anything that produces the good results that crab baits do must be worthy of special attention, and while I don't pretend that studying the biology of the shore crab has helped me to catch any more cod, it has helped me get more peelers and also keep them alive.

If you want to study the biological aspect of peeling, I suggest you apply at your local public library for the following papers. At my request photostats of the original documents were made available through the library Interloan system, so no matter where you live you should be able to get access to these most authoritative works on the life of shore crabs. The papers are: Crothers, J. H. 1967. *The Biology of the Shore Crab 1.* The background, anatomy, growth and life history. (Field Studies Vol. 2, pages 407-34). The other paper is:

Crothers, J. H. 1968. *The Biology of the Shore Crab 2.* The life of the adult crab. (Field Studies Vol. 2, pages 579–614). They are really most interesting.

The term peeler does not apply to a particular type of crab but to a stage of growth through which all crabs (and many other crustaceans) pass. As a crab's inner organs grow, the outer shell does not. When the insides become cramped the crab grows a new, larger shell underneath the existing one. When this new shell is ready, the crab discards—or peels—the old one, hence the name peeler crab. The exception is the hermit crab, which lives in old whelk shells. When the hermit finds his living quarters becoming cramped he just looks for a larger whelk shell and moves house.

The type of crab that anglers look for is the common shore crab, the type that pinches bait in the summer months. There are areas where the eating crab is found in the peeler stage, and also the white swimming crab, velvet crabs, even porcelain crabs, but in the main it is the common shore crab that anglers seek (in any event much of what follows applies to all crabs). The colour of shore crabs can vary greatly, from green to red, depending on the stage of growth and the type of ground they are living in.

The moulting process (peeling) happens about once a year on large crabs but up to three times a year with small crabs that are still growing. Upon reaching maturity—three to four years—the crabs cease to peel. The normal peeling season is from April to October, though in the warmer South West of the country crabs will peel right through winter.

The new shell is built in a corrugated, concertina-type shape underneath the old shell, and is very soft. It is largely composed of calcium which the crabs get both from the existing shell and from the calcium diffused in sea water. The extraction of calcium from the old shell is why the shell of a peeler crab is so thin and easy to break off.

When the new shell is complete, apart from the hardening process, the crab begins to take in water and expand, literally bursting its seams. The increase in volume is around thirty per cent and from the initial rupturing of the old shell to the crab crawling out takes about three hours. As soon as the crab had dragged itself out of the old shell, the hardening of the new shell begins. This hardening is done by utilising calcium stored within the body, and through absorption of calcium diffused in the sea water. It can be completed in five days, though in colder weather it can take up to sixteen days.

I do not believe that softback crabs are as effective a bait as peeler crabs as the body juices of the softback have been diluted because of the thirty per cent intake of water I mentioned previously.

To recognise a peeler crab, take hold of a leg and break off (gently) the last segment of shell. If the crab is a hardback you will see either nothing at all or perhaps a piece of white gristle. That crab is in the hardback stage and should be returned to the water. If, however, you see under the shell you remove, a perfectly formed, soft leg—coloured an orangey-brown—that crab is a peeler and is one to keep. An experienced crab angler can tell a peeler from a hardback merely by looking, because there is a slight colour change during peeling, but until you are proficient I recommend all anglers to test each crab individually. It is difficult to describe what a peeler crab leg looks like, but if you are unfamiliar, the next time you see an angler fishing with peeler crab, ask him to show you a broken leg segment.

Where to find peelers is—as any crab angler will tell you—the hardest part of all. There can't be a cod angler anywhere who wouldn't give his best rod and reel to find a place where he could get a plentiful supply of peelers the whole year round.

Unless you are one of the handful of anglers in Great Britain who have the address and the confidence of a professional peeler crab supplier, the only way you can get hold of peelers is through sheer hard work on the beach. The places to find them range from rock pools, sewer pipes, breakwaters, odd flotsam and jetsam to harbour walls—anywhere that is wet and provides cover and security for a crab while it passes through the vulnerable stage of being a peeler.

Trial and error is the best method of finding the peeler marks on your own bit of beach, but if I am landed on a strange bit of beach and want some peelers, I look for the pools of water and see if there is anything in the pool that a crab could lie under. Look for muddy areas because crabs love to sink themselves under a rock and into the mud. If you cannot overturn any likely looking obstacle, then dig your fingers into the sand surrounding the obstacle and scratch round it, feeling for crabs. A handy hint on crabbing is little rocks—little crabs. That means what is says: if there isn't much room under a rock, then there isn't much chance of finding a nice large peeler under it.

Look particularly for old tyres on the beach. These provide perfect hiding places for crabs and are easy to search. Watch out for two crabs clinging together, one on top of the other. Copulation between crabs can only take place immediately after the female crab has peeled and has a soft body. The male crab clasps the female underneath his body while the female passes through the peeling stage, so if you find two crabs in this position, the above crab will be a male and never a peeler, and the one below will be a female and usually either a peeler or a softback. You can sex a crab by looking at the triangular piece of shell to the rear of the belly. Females have a pronounced broad flap, often with corrugation, while the male has a much smaller and smoother triangle. I have never noticed any difference in the catching ability of a male peeler as opposed to a female.

Instead of searching at random on a beach, a far more successful way of collecting peeler crabs is to trap for them. If you put down places for the crabs to go when they peel, not only will you know where to go, but your returns will increase handsomely. The most popular form of trap is the car tyre and cast-iron guttering. The guttering you need is the half-moon shape, which I smash up into lengths of two to three feet. Push the guttering into a pool or a muddy hollow upside down so that one end protrudes out at an angle. With tyres the best method is to cut a hole through the tyre and pass a piece of rope through it. Tie this rope to a small stake and bury the stake in the sand as an anchor to stop the tyres being swept away.

While both these things are easily obtainable, don't overlook any odd pieces of rubbish washed up on the beach. Move them from wherever they land to a place where they might provide shelter for crabs. A few hours spent planting traps will save hours of wasted searching and without doubt increase the number of peelers you gather. Don't put all the traps so far out that you can only empty them at dead low water on big tides, remember you have to collect crabs on neaps as well as springs.

After collecting peelers, the next most important skill is keeping them alive. Unless you are going fishing immediately, or at least within hours, the ability to keep peelers alive is very important. You will never eliminate deaths entirely, but it should be no problem to keep peelers for a week, even longer. My record is nearly four weeks. The advantage of being able to keep the bait for so long is that you can have a constant supply and build up a big number of crabs if you need to.

The common shore crab is able to live out of water because the gill chambers, which are filled with water, can extract oxygen from the atmosphere as well as from sea water. The bubbling sound you hear from a bucket of peelers out of water indicates this oxygen exchange process. Should all the water in the gill chamber dry out, the crab will quickly die as the crab can't breathe. When the water dries out and the gill chamber fills with air, the crab will float, something all crab anglers have experienced at one time or another.

The most important factor in keeping peelers alive is to keep them cool. I keep mine in a fridge that is set at forty degrees fahrenheit. At that temperature the crabs are lethargic and don't waste energy, yet don't freeze to death. If the crabs are fridged as soon as they come off the beach, there is no need to give them any more attention for several days.

The box I keep my crabs in is a flat plastic box with air holes punched through the lid. I give them enough room so that they just cover the bottom of the box, though in practice they tend to climb up on top of one another. It is widespread practice to put wet seaweed in the box with the crabs or cover them with a piece of cloth soaked in seawater. I don't believe this is necessary. Weed begins to stink after a few days and I fail to see what good a damp cloth can do. They can't eat it, drink it or do anything with it, so why bother?

Every few days check the crabs and remove any dead ones. You can freeze any dead ones, but I've never had a lot of success with frozen crab. After a few days, get a bucket of sea water and dip the crabs in it for a few minutes for them to exchange the water in the gill chambers. It is vitally important that you do not leave the crabs in sea water any longer than a few minutes, or else they will start to take in the sea water to begin the peeling process.

I appreciate that keeping crabs in the fridge may not be a viable proposition for some anglers, but without keeping crabs cool in hot weather they will die within days. If you have no fridge then drape a wet blanket over them and store in the coolest place you can find.

Having spent a great deal of time in collecting and keeping

the peelers, it would be foolish to suffer heavy mortalities during the actual fishing session, as often all the crabs aren't used and those left can be returned to the fridge. It's not uncommon to see peelers stuffed in a plastic bag like marbles, thrown to the bottom of a basket under lead weights and flasks and left to bake in the sun. The best way of killing crabs I've ever come across is to keep them in a plastic bag in the sun. The bag acts like a greenhouse and the hours of work spent in getting the peelers can be wasted in no time.

I transport my crabs in a white plastic box with a wet cloth over them. This keeps them cool and prevents them being crushed. If I am going on an extended fishing trip in high summer and want to keep the crabs as cool as possible, I use a polystyrene fish box and have it fastened to the roof of the car.

We now come to the actual using of peeler crab. To find those with the most fragile and thin outer shells, look under the claw at the section of shell between the top and bottom of the crab. This is the first place to crack on a peeler and if there is a crack here, or if the shell crumbles easily under pressure, you will have a crab whose shell will easily come off.

To prepare a crab for the hook, first pull off all the legs and nippers. For cod fishing you won't need these and they can be thrown away. Then gently break off all the thin outer shell, until you are left with a legless soft ball of crab.

If the crab is bigger than a ten pence piece, cut it in half from back to front. Small crabs can be mounted whole. I always use fine cotton for whipping crab to the hook in cod fishing for two reasons. First, so that the bait is secured firmly and won't fly off during casting, and second so that should a cod pull at the bait, it won't take it off the hook but will have to come back and try again.

No knots are necessary in whipping crab to the hook. You just hold the piece of crab to the shank and bind the cotton round and round the bait until it is held tightly in position. This binding action also tends to streamline the bait and keep it clear of the hook point. To finish the whipping, just snap the cotton and it will bite into the flesh and hold fast. When rebaiting you will frequently have to cut away the old cotton, but this is no problem with a sharp knife. I advocate the thinnest and most fragile cotton you can get hold of so that when you snap it off it doesn't rip through the bait.

That sums up peeler crab fishing, and if it appears I have gone to excessive lengths in dealing with this bait, it is because it is so effective yet so mis-used and little used.

Lugworm

Lugworm catches more cod than any other bait. That is an inescapable fact of fishing because so many anglers use nothing else for cod fishing. The popularity of lugworm stems from several reasons. Firstly, there are few places where lug will not catch cod. Secondly, it is the most readily available of baits, being present on beaches right round the British Isles. Thirdly, it will keep for a considerable length of time. With three powerful reasons like that it is no wonder that for many anglers cod bait means just one thing—lugworm.

I mentioned a while back that I advocate bulk-buying syndicates for those with fresh bait problems, and I had lugworm in mind when I said that. But for those who prefer to dig their own, here's how to go about it.

Unless the lug are so spread out that digging a trench for them would give an uneconomic return—in which case I would either find a better worm bed or use a narrow spade to dig them out individually—a garden fork is the ideal tool. The best type of garden fork is a large one, capable of going deep when the worms are deep. And if you are buying a new one, look for the flat-pronged variety, sometimes referred to as a potato fork.

Locating a good lugworm bed isn't something I can write much about. Either keep your eyes open when you are fishing or ask around. To start trenching I look for a patch of casts close together, then score out the path I want to take on the surface of the sand with the fork. I usually work no wider than two forks because of the problem of flooding. Don't try and slice too much sand out at once or worms may be completely encased in the clods of sand and missed. If your trench floods, narrow the trench, if it's dry, you can go out to three or four forks wide.

If you plan to use the lug within a day or two there is little work that needs to be done to the bait other than spreading it out on a sheet of newspaper and covering it with more newspaper. Keep it as cool as possible. In summer—though I rarely use lug in summer for cod, preferring peeler crab—I keep the lug in my bait fridge. In winter the air temperature is cold enough in the garage.

If you want to keep lug longer than a couple of days, you can keep them alive for weeks by using a big tub and an aerator. I was shown this method of keeping lug by pals on Tyneside and the local record up there is three months. You have to use unpunctured worms and start off with clean seawater, but one aerator will look after a lot of lugworms. I tried the method myself to be certain it worked before including it in this book, though I have no need of it as there are millions of lug at the end of the road.

Opinions differ on the best method of hooking lug. Some head first, some tail first. Some throw the sandy tails away, some try to stop the worm bursting and some want it to burst to spread the juice downtide. I don't think it makes a scrap of difference how you hook a lug.

How many to put on the hook? It depends on the size of your lug. On a big tide I can dig the big black lug on my home beach, and they are up to ten inches long each, so half of one is a big bait. It's easier not to talk in terms of numbers on a hook, but how far up the shank and the line the worms should go, and I like to keep pushing lug on the hook until there is between one and two inches of worm above the eye of the hook (and, of course, worm covering the hook iteslf). I always leave the hook point clear on all baits.

Ragworm

Ragworm is a bait that you can't lay down rules for in cod fishing. I'm on safe ground when I say peeler crab will catch cod on all beaches and that lugworm will catch on most. But ragworm's effectiveness as a bait varies from area to area.

I don't think there are any places where ragworm will definitely *not* catch cod, but there are areas where if you asked the local angler to place baits in his order of preference, ragworm would come low down the list.

It could also be said that what I call ragworm and what is sometimes sold under that name are two different items. To me, a ragworm is bright in colour, active, and when you puncture it with a hook, it ejects a plentiful supply of dark brown liquid. That is how my ragworm look, but a lot of ragworm is sold commercially that is far removed from that description.

Ragworm sold in shops is often much-travelled, and the time it takes from digging to actually putting it on the hook shows up in the quality of the bait. Small ragworm are nice bait for flounders but when it comes to cod—nothing compares with big rag that have been freshly dug. It could well be that the reason ragworm hasn't universal appeal as a cod bait is because the type of ragworm anglers can get is sub-standard.

Whether to use ragworm as a cod bait depends largely on local reputation. If it is regarded as a good local bait, then go ahead and use it. But I don't recommend anyone to try it where general local opinion says it doesn't work.

When I talk about ragworm, I am thinking of the common red variety. That includes what is sometimes referred to as "king" rag—which is just a particularly big example of the common sort. White ragworms I shall cover shortly, and the other variety that anglers come in contact with—the tiny harbour or "creeper" ragworm—is not a cod bait.

If you wish to dig your own ragworm, finding a good bed of the worms is the first problem. The ragworm likes hard ground usually—mussels, stones and even boulders. If the area is muddy as well as hard, so much the better. The simplest way of locating a ragworm bed is to keep your eyes and ears open. The worm is often highly sought after, so it is unlikely that a good ragworm bed will get wide publicity. But if you ask around for long enough, you should find one.

The principle of digging ragworm is very similar to digging lug in that you trench for them if you are on a bed where they are plentiful. If they are not thick on the ground, try using the ragworm "shuffle" to locate individual worms. To shuffle, select an area you feel should hold ragworm and hold your feet close together. Then shuffle and stamp over the ground, watching the ground carefully. The shuffling frightens any ragworm lying close to the top of its breather hole and in contracting down the burrow, the ragworm sends a jet of water up in the air. You soon learn to recognise the ragworm squirts.

When you locate a worm you have to dig quickly. The ragworm can move very fast along its burrow and if you are slow in digging down for it you can easily miss it. I start a foot in front of the blow hole and dig back past the hole until the worm or its underground burrow is located.

To get the ragworm out of its burrow after you have uncovered part of it, don't just pull at the tail. If you do the worm will break in half. Take hold of the ragworm at least halfway along its body and hold it firm while it squirms. In this action the worm will loose itself from the burrow and you can draw it out.

Care for ragworm begins the moment you leave the beach. If you have only a very short distance to go, you can leave them in the bucket until you reach home, but if any time is involved then the moment you get the worms off the beach, spread them out on newspaper to dry.

There are two ways of keeping ragworm. The most popular is to spread them out on sheets of dry newspaper, then wrap them and store them at the bottom of the fridge. The other method is to have them crawling loose on a tray or in a flat box with a lot of seaweed. Both work satisfactorily for short periods of time (up to a week) but if you want to keep ragworm beyond a week then think about the aeration system I talked of in the lugworm part.

The amount of ragworm to use on a hook again depends on the size. Use the rule-of-thumb I suggested for lugworm of two inches above the hook.

White Ragworm

To those who have never used it—or more correctly never had any success with it—white ragworm shouldn't be any more effective a bait than red ragworm. But in practice white ragworm is one of the best baits there is for cod.

Why should white ragworm be so much more effective than red rag? If I knew definitely the answer to that question I would be a far more successful cod angler than I am. The obvious answer is that because it is white and the sea is murky, the fish can see it after they have smelled it. But that argument goes flat when you remember that white ragworm is a good bait at night.

I think, however, that the white colour of the worm does play a significant part in its attraction. So much so that I have spoken to several maggot barons in an attempt to find a dye that would change my red ragworm to white. But I have had no success. The maggot men have all pointed out that making the bait white is something they have no problem with, as it is that to start with.

The white ragworm doesn't grow nearly as big as the red

ragworm, but despite its size it is in the top bracket of cod baits.

To dig the worm depends on inside information. Not many beaches hold the white ragworm in quantities that make it worthwhile searching. If I want to get it I have to dig at random and hope. Some areas are a little more predictable but I know of nowhere where digging white ragworm is easy.

Shellfish

The use of shellfish as a cod bait is nothing like as popular as it was in years past. In pre-war and just-after days, mussel was the staple bait of the Yorkshire and North East Coast. Cockles were widely used, as were razor-fish and clams. But now their use is declining.

For a bait to decline in popularity it must mean that its efficiency as opposed to other baits is being called into question. This is, I think, what has caused the decline of shellfish. Mussel is still a fairly popular bait in Yorkshire and the North East, but fewer people now rate it higher than worm. Similarly with the cockle, which for cod fishing is used for tipping worm baits more than in its own right.

The razor-fish and the syphon clam have retained some popularity and can fish well after a blow when a natural supply of these shellfish has been washed up. But I cannot put forward any shellfish as a first choice bait for cod. So this part ends here.

Squid

I feel squid is an under-rated bait for cod, particularly when fishing from a boat. If you are fortunate enough to get hold of the imported calamaris squid, which are about six inches long, you'll be hard pushed to find something to out-fish it. Squid have a tremendous amount of smell and even if you cut lengths from a large native squid, you still have a very attractive bait.

The next time you go boat fishing for cod, tie a two-hook trace with your normal bait on one hook and a good squid bait on the other. I think you could be pleasantly surprised at what squid can catch.

If you use the large squid, don't be shy of cutting up lots of pieces, and although the bait stays intact for hours on end, change it as often as you would any other bait.

Fish Baits

When you come to the section on catching big cod you will see how highly I rate fillets of fresh fish for the big fellows. Big cod take some filling up, and whole fish makes up a large part of a big cod's diet. I've gutted dozens of cod over 20 lb., several over 30 lb. and three over 40 lb., and the stomach bag revealed mostly fish in all of them.

Fresh-caught mackerel strips make excellent baits. Frozen mackerel and herring I don't think are as effective, but at the time when a lot of cod fishing is carried on—winter—there are very few places in Britain where you can get hold of fresh mackerel.

I have not found fish baits to be very good from the shore. Worm or crab are far more effective. From a boat when you find a shoal of small codling in the 2–4 lb. range, worm will be far more successful than fish. I use fish baits when I am prepared not to catch as many as I might, but have a better chance of a big cod.

I take a complete side of a mackerel and whip it tightly to the shank of the hook, effectively making a tube shape. This bait will hold fast on the shank and not slide down to mask the point. It needs a large hook to hold this large bait and I use between 6/0 and 9/0, depending on the size of the bait I want to use. When using these very large hooks, pay extra attention to their sharpness, and if the barb is too pronounced, nip it back up slightly with pliers.

Using either live or recently dead whole fish such as pouting can be done either from the shore or from a boat. From the shore, tie a large hook to a foot of line and at the other end a link swivel. Cast out your line with just a lead on and tighten up. Then slip the snood onto the line via the link and let it slide down the line (with of course, a fish impaled on the hook). This method works best in a strong tide run, when the force of the tide will carry the bait down the line until it touches the sea bed.

You can do exactly the same thing from a boat, letting the reel line stream out from the stern, then clipping the snood on. From a boat, however, it's simpler to have the rig fixed at

the end of the line and fish in the normal way. For the hook
on a rig like this I use a treble around 4/o and hook the bait
just once through the top lip.

Hermit Crabs

The hermit crab doesn't look anything like the shore crab,
resembling if anything a lobster. Hermits live in whelk shells,
dragging their homes around with them as they forage about
in the shallow water. They are fairly widespread, but gathering
them is a problem. They never leave the sea, going in and out
with the tide, so you have to find pools or dangle a baited
drop net over the side of a pier.

Most cod anglers are more likely to come across hermit
crabs by accident while searching for something else rather
than deliberately collecting them. If you do come across one,
or fish in areas where they are fairly abundant, I strongly
suggest you try them as bait. I've had good success with them.

To get the hermit from the shell, crack it apart with a stone
and gently draw the soft abdomen out. Push the hook through
the centre of the crab bringing it out through the head, and if
you intend to cast with any power, give a few turns on it with
the bait cotton.

The biggest drawback with hermits is that they will not
stay alive out of water. They die within hours unless you keep
them in a bucket of sea water, so they really have to be used
the same day they are collected.

This bait section has not been exhaustive in that there are
a few baits I haven't mentioned that have been used to catch
cod. But there is so much choice from the list I have dealt
with that I don't see any reason for discussing highly localised
or odd baits.

I also haven't said anything about my order of preference.
If cod behaved in the same way right round the shores of
Britain, I could certainly give a list of effectiveness. But cod
vary in their likes from area to area. The best advice I can
offer is to ask around on the beach if you are unfamiliar. And
if it's your local beach you should know anyway.

As a broad generalisation, always have plenty of bait and
let it be of the best quality you can get. Change the bait or at
least add to it on every cast so that you have maximum smell.

CHAPTER THREE

Shore Fishing

Reading the beach

Reading the beach correctly is one of the blueprints of success in cod fishing. It's no good having the right bait and tackle if you are using it on the wrong beach at the wrong time. This section looks at why cod come within casting range and how you can recognise the right conditions.

It is obviously the quest for food that brings a cod close in. There are small fish, crabs, shellfish and all manner of other foods that the cod can find most abundant only in shallow water.

The common shore crab, which in summer months often forms the staple diet of cod, prefers water less than ten feet deep. In fact, below 30 ft. the shore crab is rare. Small fish such as rocklings, butterfish and gobies are also abundant in shallow water. Shellfish such as mussels, cockles and clams; the common brown shrimp; sand-eels; worms are all creatures that prefer the inter-tidal zone or just beyond. So that is the short answer to why cod choose to come within casting distance of the shore.

The above food is what can be rooted out in normal sea conditions, but should the sea become disturbed through winds or exceptional tide currents, then even more food becomes available. The surging water washes out from their hiding places the small fish and crabs and scours the sea bed, uprooting worms and shellfish. Inshore waters become even more favourable feeding areas.

This is why a lot of beaches fish best during—or just after —a heavy sea, and why a prolonged period of settled weather often spells poor cod fishing from the shore.

In areas of exceptional tidal flow (estuaries and headlands are typical examples), this churning action may be going on continually, which is why they are often less dependent on weather conditions to provide good cod fishing. Similarly, if you have an area of permanently sheltered water like the

63

Scottish sea lochs, again the fishing tends to have little relation to the weather.

I don't know of anywhere in England or Scotland where the cod fishing is noticeably better in daylight than in darkness. I can think of countless places where the reverse is true: where daylight fishing is much poorer than fishing in the dark. There is obviously a very good reason for this preference for feeding in darkness and I think it stems from a very basic instinct of the animal kingdom—fear. There is no reason to suppose that any of the inshore foods are easier to locate in darkness; in fact without the help of visual contact it must be a bit harder.

The cod has virtually no predatory enemies which is why many smaller creatures only venture out under cover of darkness. Temperature could have some bearing in the warmer months, when the daytime sun warms the inter-tidal area to beyond the tolerance of cod, but in winter when the sea temperature remains fairly constant day and night, there is still this marked difference between day and night. I cannot think of any more likely reason for this love of darkness than the natural fear of an animal.

The state of the tide frequently affects the way cod feed. There are some areas where a particular state of the tide is noted for good cod fishing and with an obvious reason. There might be little depth of water except at high tide, or a hole or gully that the average caster can only reach at low water, but there are also places where cod have a definite feeding pattern that can't be explained so simply.

Cod certainly do not feed all the time. You can know perfectly well that they are there, but no matter what bait you throw in front of them, they refuse to take it. Then, suddenly, almost as if they have been plugged in, they decide to feed as if it is going to be their last meal. Tide must have an influence here, but where?

There is a logical reason why slack water should fish poorly: there is little current in the water to carry the smell of the bait downtide. No tide action to stir up the bottom and scour out small creatures. But if a clue to the answer lies there, why should I have found a marked dropping off of sport when lure fishing at slack water?

We might also get a clue if there were a consistency in the feeding pattern, if all cod everywhere only fed freely at a certain state of the the tide. But it doesn't work like that. I know places where the first of the flood is best and where the middle of the ebb is best. It could be that the tidal feeding pattern of cod is related to the influence of tide on whatever the cod wish to feed upon, i.e. perhaps a creature stays buried except for a particular period in the tide. Or maybe a food fish shoals up tight at a certain time. Though I can't see how this idea affects the availability of shore crabs, which seem prepared to devour baits permanently!

The important thing, however, is to accept that these tidal influences on feeding patterns exist and that they are fairly predictable. Even if you don't know why the cod on a particular beach feed at a certain state of the tide within casting range, nevertheless, merely knowing that they do can help you catch them.

Although not a direct influence, the state of the tide can exercise some control over the feeding habits of the cod in that they will only feed over certain grounds at certain times. This is almost certainly linked either to the accessibility of the area (i.e. no depth until a certain state of the tide), or linked to the habits of the food in relation to the tide (i.e. whitebait moving through an area at one time only in the tide).

Think about the ground you are fishing on and try to reason out if there is a particular time in the tide when a cod would find it considerably easier to find the food. This will help you to succeed more often in putting your bait where a cod is likely to be swimming.

To move on to beach craft in particular circumstances, I'll discuss the flat sandy or shingle beach first. Whilst quite happy in fairly shallow water if there is some natural cover such as weed and rock, or better still, discolouration of the sea through wave action, the cod does not like the shallowness that, say, bass and flounders will tolerate. I wouldn't care to be definitive about minimum depths, but I think it would be unusual to find a cod feeding in less than three or four feet.

Although I refer to a beach as being flat, of course no beach is truly flat—they all have an incline of some degree, and often it is progressive, with the water getting steadily deeper the further you go out. On a beach of this type, sufficient depth to encourage cod may be at least 100 yards out, possibly more, which is why flat beaches and long casting go together. You may get them coming closer in darkness, but if you regularly fish shallow beaches from the shore, learning to cast a long way is a basic necessity.

But just as it is true to say no beach is exactly flat, neither do many beaches incline at a straight angle. There are humps, bumps and hollows. These gullies and banks are more pronounced on some beaches than others, but even if the base of the gulley is no more than a foot below the highest point of the bank, it can influence cod movement.

These gullies are where bits of rubbish and food are deposited. They are like miniature rivers, draining the beach off as the tide recedes, and as the water flows through the gulley, the heavy particles get deposited. Similarly, when the tide comes back in, it rushes through the gullies, bringing with it fresh deposits.

The things deposited in these gullies may not have a direct attraction for cod, but the gulley is a magnet for things lower down the food chain, such as crabs, shrimps, small fish and syphonic feeders such as worms and shellfish. Not only does this lower order eat the deposits, but it may well find that the non-edible things deposited or uncovered by the tide, such as stones, bits of wood and household rubbish, make excellent hiding places.

There is also the obvious attraction of a greater depth. While eventually there will be enough water over the top of a bank to encourage the cod to search there, by the time the tides reaches that stage the fish could be out of casting range.

Having noted where the gulley is while the tide is out, you should cast exactly into it when the tide is in. The simple way to do this is to mark the line by tying a tiny knot of fine line at the distance between you and the gulley. If you over-cast, you just reel in. If you back up with the tide, slide the knot along the line as you retreat. This is especially useful at night when you cannot see how far you are casting.

Breakwaters are always built across the tide and they frequently have pools round them that attract small marine creatures in the same way as gullies. However, if you intend fishing alongside a breakwater, beware of being washed into it and getting fast, or if you cast slightly beyond it, of getting swept round it. While it might be desirable to cast to the lee side of the breakwater to avoid getting washed into it, we don't all have that kind of accuracy. If your tackle lands on the opposite side to which you are standing, cross over to prevent dragging the tackle over the breakwater.

Stony areas work in a similar fashion to gullies and break-waters. They provide hiding places and food traps for small creatures.

Beware of extremes in temperature when fishing for cod on flat beaches. In summer, the hot sand will warm the water to beyond tolerance, so if there is any cod about, try for them at low water. In winter, severe frosts on the beach sends the small creatures scurrying for warmth, either by burying deep or moving out beyond the low water mark. After a prolonged period of frost, you may find that fishing at high water becomes noticeably poorer. If it does drop away, try fishing at low water.

Something you may find very useful in gaining extra distance on flat beaches is a pair of chest-high waders. Where the beach is without holes and rocks to trip you up, and providing the sea is calm, you can quite easily gain an extra 50 yards or so by wading out to waist height. If you wade out to the very limit of the waders you will find that your casting ability is severely limited because you are unable to move your body freely and have to cast holding the rod aloft. Wading out too far can also be dangerous. If the waders fill with water, you could topple over with the weight. Better to keep the depth to waist height.

I used to use chest waders extensively in competitive fishing, but in many of the matches I fish they are barred on safety ground. Fishing in any sort of crowd, you could be wading out to the area to which other anglers are casting, and you risk being hit. For this reason I don't recommend you to stay out in the water after wading out.

As you will frequently be cod fishing after a heavy sea, it's likely you will come into contact with floating weed. It can get so bad sometimes that fishing becomes near impossible because of the drag of the weed clinging to your line like a string of Monday washing. If you do get weed trouble, you might find it easier to cut the line, slide all the weed off, then knot the line. Weed is one of the drawbacks with a leader, as the weed travels down the line as you wind in, until it jams at the leader knot, forming a huge clump. The winding in operation stops as soon as the lump reaches the tip ring and you then have to drag the tackle out and remove weed from the leader knot area and from the knot where the hook snood joins the main line. You can fish with a heavy line and no leader to ease this problem, though you will obviously reduce your distance.

Try moving elsewhere on the beach. Sometimes the weed is getting washed in more in some places than others. But sometimes there's nothing to do but tolerate it or pack up and go home.

Beaches that ebb off but are of a fairly broken nature, such as those with tightly packed stones, a few larger boulders, perhaps a bed of mussels, can be looked at in a similar fashion to the plain, sandy beach in that you look for places where a cod would search for something to eat. To cope with any fastening up, you will probably have to use a fairly heavy line —let your losses be the guide to the strength of your tackle.

Whether the shallow beach is clean or broken ground, a look at the beach at low water is invaluable. To begin with, stand at the top of the beach and look at it as a whole. Scan it from left to right and study the general picture. You are looking for areas where logically a cod should go—the deeper parts or the gullies where deposited food attracts the cod. But there could be any amount of other features that could attract fish. A pool of mud, a meeting of currents, the old stumps of a long forgotten jetty, etc.

Standing on the high water mark looking at long range gives the overall picture. Having pin-pointed likely looking spots, walk down to them and take a closer look. Turn a few rocks over, stir up the bottom of the pool with your boot and see what is disturbed. A thinking approach like this doesn't guarantee you cod, but it certainly will increase your chances.

Having figured where you want to cast to, try to put your bait in exactly the right spot, don't just cast to the limit of your ability every time. Ten yards further might put you on a sand-bar. If you feel you can accurately judge where the favoured spot is, fine; if not, use the knot of line method.

It often happens, however, that you are fishing on ground that is impossible to see. Fishing at low water, deep water marks, rock edges and estuaries. Here you haven't the opportunity visually to assess the area. It is possible that the type of ground you can see above the water line is similar to that below, i.e. if you are on a rocky beach, it is reasonable to assume the rocks don't end abruptly at the low water mark; if you are on a sandy beach, the sand will continue out also.

Your own fishing experience is, of course, an invaluable guide. Not only catches, but how you found the bottom. Was it deep, shallow, clear, rough? Are there certain stretches noticeably rougher or smoother than others? Someone taking their own small boat out from the beach could give you a more accurate idea of depths and currents.

To discover a better picture of the type of ground, reel in slowly. You will soon find out if there are any unseen snags such as mussel beds, stones or weed.

To get an idea of depth you can count the seconds between the weight hitting the water and settling on the bottom. The line has a drogue effect, as does the bait, but six feet per second is a fair estimate.

In an estuary, the line of the navigational buoys can tell you where the main channel runs, and if you look at an Admiralty Chart, it will give you the minimum depths in the channel.

The Admiralty Chart can also tell you about beaches. Their descriptions are a little too general for accurate pin-pointing of potential cod marks, but they will give you a rough idea.

If the chart is a large scale one, you can discover the ground you can cover with your casting ability (with bait) by measuring from the low water mark whatever distance you can reach. On the coloured metric charts scale 1 : 50 000 one hundred yards is about five millimetres. You can draw a pencil line along the chart at whatever distance you can reach, to show clearly which areas you can reach and which you can't. If you use an Ordnance Survey map of the same area, you can pin-point exactly where on the beach you have to stand to reach the bit of water you want to fish.

It's a matter of personal opinion as to what constitutes really rough ground. Areas like Whitley Bay and Scarborough that consist of huge boulders, massive slabs of rock worn flat but criss-crossed in deep gullies and crevices, and the whole cloaked in a blanket of tough kelp and oarweed are the worst for me. The cod love ground like this, coming in close, almost to your feet as they swim through the gullies and crevices, searching out all manner of food from under the weed and rocks.

It seems as though nothing could extract fish from this type of ground, but of course many cod *are* caught here, but with the tackle to compete with—never beat—the conditions. I described the type of tackle to use on this type of ground earlier in the book, so here I'll discuss which lump of kelp or rock pool to fish in.

Although these areas produce cod at high water, low water when the angler can walk out onto the fringes of the kelp beds is better. If you are unfamiliar with this style of fishing, take great care as you walk out over weed-covered rocks and cross flooded gullies. It is quite common for a gulley to be a couple of feet wide and six feet deep. The gullies have been formed through faults in the rock, so they take the form of deep splits, and a careless footing can get you a soaking . . . or worse. Studded boots are essential for walking on weed-covered rocks. Ordinary rubber soles slip and slide.

Whenever there is any kind of a sea running on rock edge, you get "splash-ups", which is the sea hitting the edge of the rock and flying up. Don't stand near the edge of the rock or you can get knocked over, and you'll keep drier if you wear a bib and brace over-trousers set as well as waders.

The rougher the sea, the more the bottoms of these gullies get churned up, dislodging the small creatures that the cod are looking for. This is why the howling easterly winds are so beloved in the North East. If you have a choice, always opt for the gulley or pool that is the roughest. It is invariably where most cod will be. Unless you know the area very well, have a good look at low water to see where the gullies run, which ones dry out and which keep a good depth of water even at very low water.

In spite of the vast amount of natural cover by way of weeds and rocks, the cod in these rough areas still come inshore in greater numbers when the water is coloured. Once stirred up, the water will remain discoloured for two or three days after a blow, and this after-period as the sea begins to settle down, is the peak time for rock edge fishing. It is the only time daylight fishing can compare with night fishing, though in periods of settled weather, darkness is far superior.

An inescapable problem with fishing over rough ground is getting fast on the bottom. It is bound to happen sooner or later, but you can lessen the chances by reeling in as fast as you can (high-speed reel very useful) so as to get the lead and trailing hooks clear of the bottom as soon as possible. Once you begin reeling in, you must keep the same speed up, even if there is a lively codling trying to stop you. If you relax, even in the last few yards the fish can dart sideways, taking the line round an obstruction, or the weight can fall to the bottom and lodge in a crevice or round a rock.

Also avoid the temptation to keep tightening up the line

70

during fishing. When you first cast in, stop the line as soon as the weight hits the water. As the weight falls, it will take up the slack line before it hits the bottom. If you do get a lot of slack, take it up very slowly so the weight is not moved.

If you do get fast, and a good hard heave fails to budge the tackle, let off slack line. This releasing of pressure on the weight may allow it to fall clear of the obstruction. A few moments after releasing the line, jerk the weight as hard as you can to try to pull it over the obstruction. Alternatively, slacken the line off again and walk ten or fifteen yards to the right or left, still with the line slack. Then tighten up the slack and yank hard again to try to pull the tackle sideways away from the obstruction.

If you have a fish on, giving it slack line may encourage it to drag the weight clear, you may lose it, but there isn't any alternative if you are fast solid. If all else fails, wrap the line round an arm or shoulder so that the pressure is taken off the reel, and walk back with the line until either the tackle comes free or the line parts. Don't just pull on the line with the reel taking the tension, or you will force the line to cut deep into the spool and jam tight. The next time you try to cast you will have terrible trouble.

The use of a weaker length of line for attaching the weight to the tackle, called in the North East a "rotten bottom", isn't a must for this heavy ground fishing, but without it you stand to lose more tackle and probably fish than if you do use one. However you tie up your trace, the weight has a piece of line (length immaterial, but I recommend six inches) about twenty-five per cent weaker than the rest of the line. If the weight gets fast, the tackle will break at the weakest point—that short weak link—and the hook, and possibly the fish, will come free.

On my Scarborough centre pin I have 55 lb. line and use 35 lb. weak links. That keeps tackle losses down to a tolerable level.

The best piece of general advice on locating cod is to keep on the move. If you have done your homework on the beach, are casting to the spot where logically the cod should be but they are not, don't just sit there puzzling, get up and move to another likely spot. There might be half a dozen possible places on a beach where the cod might be feeding. Unless there is a great quantity of cod about, they can only be in one spot at a time, and might remain in that spot the whole tide.

So always have a few alternatives in mind if your first choice spot draws a blank.

You don't have to move a very long way either. A couple of hundred yards may be enough to find the cod. It is also possible that you can scare a shoal of cod off by the number you take from it and the splashing about of your tackle landing in the water and dragging fish out. Every now and then, when your luck's in, you can drop on a shoal and take fish from the start. Bites every cast and it seems as though all your birthdays have come at once. After an hour or so the fishing may ease back—there may not be so many and the bites may be less positive.

A number of things could have happened to cause that. The fish could have just moved off quite naturally; there aren't any left; or you have spooked them. If you move, you could be going where there aren't any cod at all, or you could be moving back onto the fish. It's a gamble whatever you do, but it can pay good dividends if your number comes up.

Casting

The intense passion with which many anglers talk about casting ability never ceases to amaze me. It almost seems as if for some people the point of the exercise is not to catch a fish but to outcast everyone else on the beach.

More frustration and bad tempers are caused by casting problems than any amount of lost fish and missed bites. To some, prowess is measured not in pounds of fish flesh but in yards between yourself and your lead. Casting in its own right, with just a lead and on a remote field or beach can be a pleasurable exercise in itself. Apart from the obvious pleasure of knowing you are master of your equipment, this field practice will help achieve smoothness and (if you need it) distance.

But never believe that at all times the further you can cast the more you will catch. Casting is an important part of shore fishing for cod, but no more so than having the right bait or being on the beach at the right time.

Distance casting is vital in some areas, helpful in others and a downright handicap in a few. To cast a long way over rough ground is courting disaster. You might get plenty of bites and hook the fish, but you will have the devil of a job trying to get the fish in across all that rough without heavy tackle and fish losses. In areas like this you have to short cast, and to some-one educated to believe distance equals fish, casting short can be harder than casting a long way. A great many anglers fish at only one distance the whole time—the farthest they can throw.

This chuck-as-far-as-you-can brigade seem to believe that (a) all beaches descend at a fixed incline, getting progressively deeper the further they go out, and (b) that cod are stacked in a flat pyramid fashion with the least number close in and the most farthest out. This situation exists on some beaches, and undoubtedly the further you throw out, the greater your chances is the rule. But the angler who reads the beach and puts his bait where the cod are likely to be irrespective of how far out it is, will, over a season, fare better than the fellow who parks himself anywhere and throws out blindly, but a long way.

The purpose of this preamble to the casting section has not been to discourage anyone from improving their casting ability but to warn of the dangers of becoming obsessed with distance. And having said that, I'll go into the mechanics of casting.

Simply, we are transferring the energy from our muscles into the weight, but doing it in a way that makes the most of use of our muscle power. The medium through which the muscle power passes to the weight is the rod, so we want a rod that will absorb every ounce we put in, yet will use only a minimum amount and pass on as much energy as possible into the weight. When the weight receives the energy, it uses it in the only way it can—by flying through the air.

The more energy we can put into the rod (compression), the greater the distance the lead will travel. It is to get maximum compression that the circular-style casts used on tournament fields—and beaches—were developed because with the still widely used overhead cast there isn't enough time or oppor-tunity to compress a rod to the limit of an angler's ability.

The longer the time from first starting the cast to releasing the lead, the more time you have to build up greater compres-sion into the rod. Look at the two stick men in Figure 11. In the overhead cast stick man (a) is doing, he has just that 90 degree angle in which he can compress the rod. But stick man (b) who is bringing the lead round his body before releasing the lead, has three times the area of stick man (a) in which to build up power. The last part of stick man (b)'s cast is similar to the overhead cast of (a), but whereas (a) has a static start, (b)'s rod is already under compression and still absorbing power by the time he reaches the overhead cast start point.

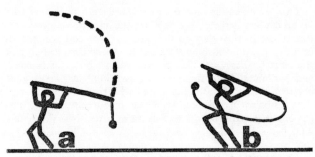

FIG. 11. These two stick men illustrate the movement of the inefficient overhead cast (a), and circular cast (b).

The three most popular tournament styles are: the pendulum, the Yarmouth and the South African, and all three in varying degrees involve a circular movement of the lead. The pendulum cast achieved its first widespread popularity through the records created by Nigel Forrest. As the ideal rod length for this style is between 11 ft. and 12 ft., it is the style best suited to most production rods.

The Yarmouth style has its history tied into the centre pin and Scarborough reel style of casting, so not surprisingly, the Yarmouth, as it is popularly known, is the basic style of casting up in the North East where centre-pin reels are still popular today. There are many similarities between the Yarmouth and the pendulum, but the basic difference is that the power stroke in the Yarmouth is a pulling action, whereas the pendulum is both pulling and pushing.

The South African style in its true form isn't very practical for fishing on a crowded beach because it involves taking a big stride—almost a jump—along the beach and dragging your weight through the sand. Hardly the ideal method on a weed-covered rock edge in darkness! The dragging and sudden leap are to give an initial compression to the rod at the start of the cast.

The basic style of the South African cast is to hold the rod parallel to the sea and lay the lead on the ground so that there is a straight line from weight to reel. After the initial dragging, the rod is swept round the body and over the shoulder. While good distances can be cast with both the Yarmouth and South African styles, with rods of 11 ft. to 12 ft., greater distances can be achieved with a length of 13 ft. to 14 ft. This is a length not normally found in production rods, so the anglers who want this length make their own from a one-piece tip section of fast-taper hollow glass around 100 inches long, then butt on dural tube for the total rod length they want.

All three styles can be used with either multiplier or fixed spool reels and with any normal surf-casting weight. All three styles are potential record-breakers so there is no reason to perfect more than one style. And perfection is what you have to go for if you really want to hit big distances. No matter what you read or how much you spend, the only way to get smooth, trouble-free long casts is to practise.

Not only do you have to practise, but practise correctly. If your current technique is jerky and basically wrong, no amount of practise will make life easier. All you will do is get very profficient at over-runs.

Before I get on to the actual casting, I'll recap and enlarge on what I said about reels in the earlier tackle section. Whilst in terms of tournament distances, you need a small light reel like the Abu 6500, it is quite possible to cast in excess of 150 yards with larger reels such as the Abu 7000 and 9000C. It's just that little bit easier with the smaller reels.

No matter what your choice of reel is, when you first begin to try and cast long distances you will need some kind of drag on the spool. To cast baited tackle without any spool brake needs a very smooth cast, a steady build-up of power with no sudden jerks. It will take a great deal of practice to reach this level of perfection, so in the meantime you will save temper and line by having a braking system on the spool.

There are four ways in which a brake can be applied to the spool during the cast. You can thumb the spool, slowing it by applying pressure either all the time or as soon as you hear bunching. This is most unsatisfactory as it is an abrupt brake that slows the spool down too much. When you release the pressure, the lead jerks forward and starts the spool spinning too fast again.

Another way is to tighten up the spindle bearing—the

knurled nut in the centre of the side plate opposite the handle. This is a smooth braking system but will cause wear on the bearings and on the spindle on the spool. I used this method many years ago on a Penn Squidder and found I had to keep tightening up the nut until it was fully home and the spool still slack. The spool was then useless.

The third way of spool braking is via an inbuilt braking system, either centrifugal brake blocks as on the Abu reels or vanes on the inside of the spool as in the Penn Squidder. This is a good way of braking the spool as it involves no wear and in the case of the brake blocks, can be adjusted by varying the number of brake blocks in the reel from two to none. When I first began casting in earnest, I started with both brake blocks intact. Then I reduced it to one, and when I ceased to have any trouble with one, did without any at all. However, whilst your casts may be trouble free using brake blocks, they restrict your distances.

The fourth and most efficient method of spool braking is by using lubricants, which not only make the cast smoother, but when you use oils of a thicker viscosity, will give a smooth and continual braking action. The beauty of using oil and grease as a brake is that you can control it to a fine degree by mixing oils to whatever viscosity you want.

I use a lubrication system given to me by Tony Allen, of Norfolk, and I reproduce it here. This explanation is based on the Abu 6500, but can be adapted for most other casting reels.

"Strip the reel apart and remove the roller bearings. Soak them in petrol for half an hour, stirring them about to dislodge the grease. Remove the bearings from the petrol and spin them on a match and dry them off on a paper towel. Warm some SAE 90 oil in a small container, warm not hot, drop the bearings in and if small air bubbles come up, you know oil has penetrated into the bearings. Wipe excess oil off after ten minutes and put them back into the reel.

"Use a dab of STP oil, which is thick, on the end of each spindle to slow the reel down while you practise casting. As you get proficient with the reel, getting no over-runs, you can substitute the STP for SAE 90 oil in the check side of the spool and then on the drive side."

That is the method I use and it enables me to put a lead in excess of 180 yards with a Cono-Flex rod and Abu 6500 multiplier.

The only other adjustment to the reel is to adjust the spool play by tightening or slackening the end nut on the side plate (check side) until there is just a perceptible amount of play. Never have it sloppy or over-tight.

The level wind mechanism on a multiplier (where fitted) is a great help in keeping the line evenly distributed on the spool. If you are bringing a fish in and are worried about losing it, you have enough problems without having to make sure the line is evenly wound onto the spool so as to prevent trouble at the next cast. But there is no doubt that a level-wind will restrict your distance simply because the winder is permanently in gear, even when you are casting. The loss of power isn't as great as perhaps some might imagine, but it is there and measurable.

There is another problem with level winds and that is when the leader knot is flying through it at great speed. If the knot hits the side of the level wind at a bad angle, it will stop long enough to part the leader from the main line. You can often hear this banging as you cast, even if the line doesn't part. The problem is multiplied even further should a bit of weed get tangled up round the leader knot, or if a substantial amount of weed collects at the knot when you are reeling in and jams at the level wind. For a reel to stop here is the most dangerous time of all with a cod on, because the fish will still be fighting against your lighter main line yet be right in the surf with its powerful drag force. If this should happen, don't try to clear the leader knot, but immediately grasp the leader and walk back up the beach and drag the cod clear by hand.

For this reason the level wind mechanism is removed on my Abu 6500 and 6000. When the time comes for me to replace one of them I shall hopefully try to get one of the limited edition 6500CT reels which were primarily designed for the tournament caster. They are the standard reel but without the level wind mechanism. If you remove the level wind from your reel, you will have two holes left in the body of the reel where the level wind bar previously fitted. Seal these holes up either permanently with a flat piece of plastic Araldited into position, or temporarily with waterproof sticking plaster.

There is a further modification you may wish to make on small reels like the Ambassadeurs, and that is to remove the top crossbar so that you can get your thumb further round the spool to prevent it dragging from under your thumb during a cast. This is a solid bar and you will have to cut it off with a hacksaw. You are obviously weakening the reel, but since I did mine I have had no trouble with distortion. The positioning of the crossbars on small Ambassadeurs is something I think could be improved by Abu. On the 6500CT this crossbar has been moved further round the reel.

The strength of main line above which you have to use a leader depends on your style of casting and how much power you put into it. Most anglers will have problems of smashing the line with strengths under 25 lb. breaking strain. But if you do decide to cast without a leader, be certain that you are confident you will not smash off. If a lead were to break off during casting, fly off and hit someone, the result could be like a dum-dum bullet. Remember the continual weakening of line in the last few yards as you continually cast with it. Don't take chances with other people's lives.

To attach a leader to the main line there are a number of knots. The blood knot is unsatisfactory because that only works properly with lines of a similar diameter. You can reduce the diameter of your leader at the point where you intend to knot it by drawing it through fine glass paper. You get a flat shape instead of a tapering point, but providing you don't go too thin, the leader will still be stronger than the main line. A side effect of this is that the final knot will be smaller, too.

A knot popular on the tournament field is the needle knot. You hammer flat the end of the leader and poke a hole through it with a fine needle. You then attach the main line by passing it through the hole and tying an ordinary half blood with a tuck.

The knot I use is a whipping knot, as used for tying spade end hooks to line. Figure 12 shows how it is tied. The knot in the end of the leader is a plain overhand knot—the over-and-under knot that you use for tying shoe-laces with. It is pulled as tight as possible and clipped close to the knot. The number of turns should not be less than five. Just before you pull it tight, slide the knot down to the knot on the end of the leader. You can trim this knot fairly close, and don't forget to wet the knot before tightening it.

You need only three turns of a leader on the reel to withstand the shock of casting, and you can carry spare leaders already knotted at the end in your bag. I recommend not less than 40 lb. breaking strain line for leaders. Avoid going too heavy for leaders because you will create a very bulky knot that can jam against a ring.

To describe how to cast by using words is extremely difficult. Talk of shifting body weight, positions of the body in relation to a clock face, do little but compound the confusion many anglers already have about distance casting.

Instead, I shall outline the principle of long casting. Look back at the stick men in Figure 11. It's a very simple drawing but it emphasises clearly the right and wrong shapes of cast. stick man (b) has got the principle right and that is how all casts should be constructed. You can develop your own variation on this basic movement to suit your build and rod length but as long as that sweep round is there you are on the way to casting a long way.

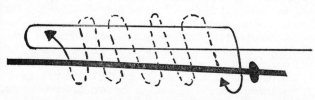

FIG. 12. This is the knot I use for fastening a leader to the main line. An ordinary overhand knot is pulled very tight into the end of the leader. Then double the main line back as shown, and whip it a minimum of five turns back up itself, finishing off by passing the end of the main line through the loop indicated by the arrow. Before pulling anchor-tight, slide the knot down the leader so that it nestles up against the knot in the leader. This knot can be trimmed quite close.

The drop is the distance from tip to weight and for most anglers on a flat beach 8 ft. is about right. On a steep-sloping beach you may have to shorten this drop if the weight bangs on the ground.

Most casts will be improved by starting with the body leaning forward slightly and by getting the weight to swing towards you and away from you like the pendulum of a grandfather clock. Commence the power stroke when the weight is nearest to you.

A common fault of anglers who are attempting to cast a long way is to start off well with a flowing action, but at the end of the cast they suddenly jerk, as if mistakenly believing that distance requires tremendous power and speed. Great distances demand that, but 140 yards can be achieved with a remarkable lack of speed and power.

Bite detection

The commonest way to detect a bite is to put the rod on a rest and stand watching it. When the rod tip shakes, it means a cod is pulling the bait, so you pick the rod up and strike it. A variation of this when fishing on rocky ground is to lodge the butt of the rod in a crevice, or lean it on a rock. The type of rod rest depends on local fancy as much as local conditions, anglers in the same area all tending to opt for a similar design. The two basic shapes of rod rest are tripods and monopods. The tripod is the stand-alone, three-legged type, and the monopod is the spike type that you drive into the beach. The advantage of the monopod is that on beaches where there is a heavy surf, because the rod is lifted high, the first few breakers are missed, so easing the problem of tide pull being mistaken for bites.

The big disadvantage of not having the rod in your hands at the moment a take is signalled, is the time lag between your seeing the bite and picking up the rod and striking. Many anglers who use rod rests rely on the double take. They see the first bite on the rest, then position themselves ready to snatch the rod at the next bite, or possibly take hold of the rod and wait for the cod to come again. The idea works as long as the cod are coming back for a second and third try, but many times you don't get a second chance. The cod bump once, then get frightened off. No one could argue that hitting the bite the first time is the best method.

Another drawback with rests occurs in night fishing. You have to peer at the tip through the flickering light of a Tilley lamp, torch or headlamp, and the strain can make your eyes play tricks and hurt with the strain. Watching a tip at night is definitely hard work.

By far the most satisfactory methods of bite detection involve holding the rod in some way. Then you can strike as soon as you believe the cod has the hook inside its mouth.

There are two basic variations to this method. One, you put the butt on the beach against your foot and grip the rod somewhere round the centre. This method is useful where there is a heavy pull on the rod through strong currents or heavy seas, where to take all the strain of the pull in your arms will soon make them ache. The other method is to hold the rod in two hands in a position that makes the line go at a right angle when it leaves the tip ring.

In this method you are feeling for a shuddering in the rod that is different from any tide action vibration. This is one instance where the written word is no substitute for experience. But while difficult to describe, once you have held your rod and felt bites, you quickly learn to tell them apart from other forces. Sight can also play a part in this method of bite detection by watching the rod tip as well as feeling the glass.

Apart from the common bite of a rapid series of jerks, also watch out for slack line bites. These are caused by the cod picking up the bait and running inshore with it and dragging the weight. If the tension suddenly disappears from the rod, step smartly back and if there is still no tension, hit the bite hard. If you are on a clean beach, run backwards until you feel the tension, then hit the hook home. Never do this on a stony or slippery beach or you can end up flat on your back. The only way you can hit slack-liners on rough beaches is to reel in for all you're worth until the tension comes back, then hit the hook. As you reel, lower the rod tip to the horizontal position, then you can strike by lifting the rod high over your head.

There are times when I use a rest and times when I hold the rod with the line at right angles, but most times I use a completely different principle of bite detection. I call it fingering, though in freshwater fishing it is called touch-legering.

The rod plays no part in the bite detection: it is all to do with feeling the line. I tuck the rod under an arm and point in the direction in which the line is going, so that as near as possible there is a straight line from reel to bait. I then crook the line round the thumb and fore-finger so that the line passes over the ball of the fore-finger. When the fish pulls on the line, it registers on the finger instead of on the rod.

The sensitivity of the finger-tip is incredible. Just try to touch the surface of the finger-tip without being able to feel anything. Unless you've got very calloused fingers it's impossible. Another advantage of this method of bite detection is that you are standing in a position which enables you to get the maximum lift of the rod to set a hook.

Night fishing isn't any different from daylight fishing, as

C.F.—D

sight plays no part in this method of bite detection. It is also better in windy weather because of the sensation of the line blowing from side to side isn't anything like the feel of a definite pull.

You can prop the rod on top of a tripod rod rest to take the weight of the rod and reel, so that you can stand for hours with no strain at all. Where bites are very shy, fingering will easily beat any other form of bite detection.

But the method does have its drawbacks. One is in very cold weather when the fingers go numb and you have to change your method of bite detection. You can obviously keep your fingers warm with gloves, but they have to be thin or too much sensitivity is lost. The method also fails in places where you cannot point the rod in the direction of the line, such as boat fishing and fishing from piers or high cliffs.

No matter what method of bite detection you use, there is one problem common to them all: when to strike. If we all could hit every bite we get, what a lot of cod we'd catch! Think about how a bite is created. The cod picks up the bait and moves off with it in its mouth. The pull is registered on the rod and we lift the rod to jerk the hook into the flesh of the cod's mouth.

Something more than a gentle swim must be happening because cod bites are not just long, slow pulls which is the reaction you would get if the fish was simply moving off with the bait. The tip invariably shakes jerkily, which means that the cod must be moving its head in staccato fashion. Possibly it has the bait in its mouth, has felt a resistance and is shaking its head to free the bait from whatever is holding it. Rather in the way one would imagine a cod would try to dislodge a crab from a crevice, a worm from its burrow, etc.

While the cod is shaking the bait and pulling it, the hook is obviously in its mouth, so this is the time to hit the bite. Speed, then, is important in hitting bites. As soon as it is clear that the bait is in the cod's mouth, hit fast and hit hard. Remember how much stretch you have in your fishing line, so the bigger the sweep of the rod the better. What you must not do is to be frightened of striking in case you miss the bite. To hesitate is more likely to cost you the fish than striking too soon.

Too many anglers want to wait for that giant yank (which probably means the cod has hooked itself anyhow) rather than risk striking at the wrong time. If you practise striking long enough and think about the times when you strike, you can develop this into an almost instinctive reaction. I'll repeat those rules of striking: as soon as the bait is taken, hit fast and hit hard. Only if you are certain that the cod are not taking the bait properly need you delay striking and wait for further pulls.

As soon as you strike and you feel the solid resistance of a fish, start reeling in straight away with the rod tip high in the air. Slack line immediately after the strike could allow the fish to shake the hook free if your strike hasn't set the hook home properly. But as soon as you begin to reel in, the fish pulling against you will set the hook home. The rod is held high to act as a buffer for any sudden movements of the fish, especially when fishing with light lines.

Don't stop reeling until the fish is on the beach or someone is behind it. If you are fishing in heavy surf, try to gauge it so that the fish is dragged from the sea with the help of a wave surging forward. If you try to drag the cod through the first big breaker when it is washing back down the beach, the extra drag and undertow can literally rip the fish from the hook. If weed round the leader knot suddenly prevents you from reeling in the last few yards, walk backwards (if safe to do so) so that the pressure is not eased off at this critical time.

While all your mind should be concentrating on getting the fish in, if you are using a multiplier without a level wind, train your fingers instinctively to spread the line evenly so that you don't get problems the next time you want to cast.

Cod in Match Fishing

It is, perhaps, unusual to include a chapter on competitive fishing for cod, but so many do it—3000 in the 1975 match organised by the Northern Federation of Sea Anglers—that I think it warrants a small section to itself.

Basically, there isn't a lot of difference between a well-planned pleasure trip for cod and an attempt to win a match with them. On both occasions you are trying hard but in a match you are not only trying to catch cod, but to catch a greater weight of them than anyone else.

A growing number of shore matches are run on a roving basis these days, so the first problem is choosing your spot. Is it any different from choosing your spot for a pleasure trip? Definitely. On a typical cod beach there are well-known hot spots—the hole, gulley, rocky ground, etc. The kind of place you would make for automatically if you were going fishing on your own.

But the snag is that a couple of hundred other anglers might have the same idea. A spot that comfortably holds half a dozen anglers will fish very differently with a hundred hopefuls throwing baits in it. This is why so many matches seem to be won not in the hot spot but the odd spot. Another reason winning catches often come from unexpected places is that anglers are obliged to fish in places they wouldn't normally bother with—and get a pleasant surprise.

Back to the hot spot of the match. If we discount the possibility of the cod being frightened off by so much lead banging in around them and members of the shoal suddenly heading mysteriously towards the shore, we must all agree that there are only so many cod out there to be caught. I'll give an example of what I mean.

In Bloggs Hole (the hot spot) there are fifty cod feeding and waiting to be caught. On your own you'd have a beano of a time, maybe get a dozen or so. But on match day there are a hundred anglers fishing Bloggs Hole, all throwing the same bait in the same spot, so on average all will get half a codling each. That being impossible, some will get two or three and some will get none. Perhaps one angler fishes exceptionally well and gets four. At the end of the day Bloggs Hole has produced just as many fish as it would normally have done, but they have been shared out among many anglers.

Way down the beach there is another known cod spot, Fred's Gulley. Everyone knows that while Fred's Gulley is a fair old spot for cod, it's nothing like as productive as Bloggs Hole, so few competitors have gone there. There are only twenty-five cod feeding in Fred's Gulley, just half as many as in Bloggs Hole, but only five anglers thought it worth trying.

Working on the same principle of sharing the fish out, each of the anglers in Fred's Gulley will get five codling each. But in practice it won't work out like that because a couple of the anglers will get hardly any cod and a couple will get more than average, say six or seven, and the match is going to be won in Fred's Gulley.

At the weigh-in, the anglers who opted for Bloggs Hole will shake their heads and wonder why it fished so badly. It didn't, of course. It's just that the fish were shared out among a greater number of anglers.

The aim of that story is to show that when it comes to match fishing it isn't always the most obvious choice spot that provides the best weights, and how by opting for a place of lesser repute but having it to yourself you can outfish the best.

If you do any amount of competitive fishing you will from time to time be faced with the problem of figuring out where to fish on a beach you've never seen before. Normally, I would say just apply what I discussed in the beachcraft section. Read the beach and deduce where the cod are likely to be. But as I explained, cod don't always work as methodically as the angler. They may not be in the place they logically should be. The cod will be in one of (say) three places on the beach. When you fail to catch in the first hour, you move on. If you fail to catch in the second hour, you move on, and in the third hour you find them. The trouble is it's only a three-hour match so you're snookered.

This is why the professional approach to competitive shore fishing is to go the day before and fish the identical times (allow for the difference in tide times) so that even if it takes you three or four hours to find where the cod are in practice, come the match you can sit right on top of them from the off. If you are travelling in a group who are all competent anglers so much the better because you can split up on practice day and cover the whole match venue. The edge this pre-match practice gives you is immense.

There are times, however, when even the keenest of us cannot afford the time to go the day before and we have to rely on the judgment we can apply on the morning of the match. Apart from using your own evaluation of the venue by touring it from end to end, walk about the registration point and keep asking questions. Ask as many anglers as you can where they think the match is going to be won.

You usually get either an honest answer or an evasive one. Rarely a downright lie. You may get a variance of opinion, but if you ask enough people, you can narrow down the choices. Also don't forget to ask the match officials, who probably won't be fishing and will be pleased to see strangers to their match and be only too willing to help.

The first time I ever fished the Hornsea Open in Yorkshire I used this method of evaluation and after narrowing the options down to three I then used my own judgment to weigh up the beach . . . and won the match with two cod and a bonus flounder.

Had I been fishing normally on this beach I doubt that I would have caught that flounder because my hooks would have been too large for it to manage. But you must expect and indeed hope for little codling as well as big ones in a match, and providing the hook point is not masked, a small hook will catch a big cod as well as a small one, but a big hook will make catching small codling difficult. Of course there is the bonus of small fish other than cod like the flounder, or whiting or pouting, dabs, etc. I rarely go above a 3/0 in competitive cod fishing. Often I use a 1/0, and I can't recall ever losing a fish because I used a hook smaller than normal.

Remember also that you are out to beat several hundred other anglers who should be as keen as you to take the honours, so spare nothing in the way of tackle and bait. To be the best on the day you have to *be* the best. It's no fluke that the same faces are seen trotting up to the prize table every other match. It's the bloke you saw fishing the day before in all that rain . . . the one going out digging bait as you went for a pint to talk about catching cod instead of doing something practical about it.

CHAPTER FOUR

Boat Fishing

To start off this boat fishing section I'll discuss the two basics: the rod and reel. Of the two I would say there are more bad boat rods on the market than bad beach rods. The commonest fault with a boat rod is the ferrules, which under strain just fold over. Cheap, imported rods seem particularly prone to this. I have also seen rods where the join is via the wooden handle, pull out of the handle and break off because the glass has not been sunk far enough into the handle for cost-saving.

The simplest way of preventing ferrule damage is not to have one at all, but to have one-piece boat rods. You will have no problems with rods at the expensive end of the market, but beware of cheap boat rods. They aren't worth it.

A far better proposition is to buy a quality blank from a reputable blank stockist and make up the rod yourself. With all the bits in front of you and excluding the varnishing, you can put a rod together with reel fittings and rings in under an hour.

For the price of a boat rod of doubtful quality you will have a rod of the best glass available.

Boat rod lengths seem to average out at 6 ft., and that's quite functional. However, I prefer 7 ft. to 7 ft. 6 in. for two reasons. The longer the rod the more lift you can put into the strike, and this is especially important in deep water fishing. With a rod of 7 ft. 6 in. you have just as fast a strike as with a short rod. A longer rod is better for lure fishing as the extra lift you get from the extra length allows you to work a greater range on the bottom and keeps the lure more active.

Boat rods are now being sold with reference to the breaking strain of line they are best suited to. The International Game Fish Association (IGFA) classes, which are accepted by a lot of other fishing organisations, are: 6 lb., 12 lb., 20 lb., 30 lb., 50 lb., 80 lb., 130 lb. and "all tackle". Each line strength has its own record list, so anglers interested in this type of record hunting, first buy the line then a rod that has optimum performance with the maximum pressure the line can exert.

Thus a 30 lb. class outfit is a line of *less* than 30 lb. breaking strain, on a rod that with the maximum pressure 30 lb. line can exert, performs well, not losing power or sensitivity.

The "class" of a rod can be a guide when buying either a blank or a made-up rod, though it is largely left up to the manufacturer as to what constitutes a 30 lb. blank, it is possible to get two rods labelled as 30 lb. class but which have noticeably different actions. IGFA also say that for a rod to be eligible for their record list it must not be less than 6 ft. 5 in. long.

The choice of "class" depends on how you like your fishing. If you want to see the rod bumping hard with a nice curve from a lively six-pounder, and providing you are not in deep water or heavy tide run, then try a 12 lb. class outfit.

A good all-round rod is the 20 lb. class, which is easily heavy enough to cope with the energy of most cod and will stand use in fast currents. If you are in deep water or having to use a lot of lead to hold bottom, you might be more comfortable with a 30 lb. class rod, which will cope not only with the next record cod but with all but the most severe sea conditions.

If you start going into the 50 lb. class of rod, not only will it require a cod of over 20 lb. even to flex the thing, but I believe a broompole rod can cause you to lose fish.

One of the properties a good boat rod should have is to act as a buffer for any sudden jerking by the fish. Rods in the 20 lb. class have a perfect cushioning effect, and should the cod make a sudden rush near the surface, it is slowed down gradually. If there is no cushioning effect, as there isn't with broompole rods, then that sudden jar can rip the hook from the fish's mouth. I've seen this happen several times in lure fishing, with the cod shaking its head just on the surface and ripping the hook free.

The choice of a reel to match the rod isn't that critical. Fixed spool reels are definitely out as their high ratio and method of retrieve, which involves the line being dragged round a right angled bend, make fishing awkward.

The multiplier is the obvious choice for boat fishing, and for cod fishing I don't think the choice is critical. Use one with a burst-proof spool and if you are using light lines, make it a force of habit to check the drag at the start of each trip to see that if something should make a powerful run, line will slip. If you are in the 12 lb. class, the small Abu multipliers are perfect. In 20 lb. and 30 lb. you can use with confidence your normal beach reel, though possibly with a spare spool (burst-proof) loaded with the line to match the rod you are using.

Unkind shore fishermen sometimes refer to boat fishing as the lazy way of fishing. Not only is that idea unkind, it is also very inaccurate. Certainly boat fishing attracts anglers whose ability and interest is limited, but so, too, does shore fishing. While to some, boat fishing may be an escape route for those who can't cast, to me it's every bit as skilful as good shore fishing.

Identical in both shore and boat fishing is the need to locate the right mark. The shore angler reads the beach—the boat angler the Admiralty Chart. Bait is the same, and end tackle is similar. Both can have problems with strong tides and rough ground. In fact the only difference between the two is casting. You don't have to bother with it in a boat.

I shall discuss boat fishing for cod in general and separate small boat fishing from charter boat fishing.

To get to your mark by charter boat you have to find a good skipper with a good boat (the two usually go together) and to get good cod fishing you have to be there at the right time. This last point is the problem for many boat anglers. Locating a good skipper isn't too difficult of you read carefully the Angling Press and chat on the quayside to other anglers. The problem is getting a booking with the good skipper at a time when the cod are showing well. Successful skippers are booked up well in advance for week-end trips and if you want to get a week-end booking when conditions are perfect you may have to be prepared to book twelve months in advance.

To establish contact with the skipper, ring him up and explain that your group or club wish to charter his boat for a day's cod fishing. Tell him that you don't mind having to wait a long time to get the right day. Ask him which week-end he would recommend for the best chance of a good day's cod fishing. Tell him you don't mind a very early start or a late finish, or having to spend more time than usual travelling out to distant grounds.

What you are doing is showing the skipper that you are a bunch of keen anglers who want the best from the skipper and his boat. If you ask polite, intelligent questions the skipper will respond. That is the way to get a good day's cod fishing.

If you are fishing from your own small boat, you will often be limited in the range at which you can fish because of safety considerations and your lack of navigational equipment. Fishing in small boats can be great fun but very dangerous if your knowledge of seamanship and the quality of your outfit are not up to scratch. Small boat safety could be the subject of a book in itself, so rather than skimp over it I advise anyone who feels they are lacking in this department to read a specialist book on the subject. And never take chances.

To find your best marks you need Admiralty Charts of the area you intend to fish, and if you enquire at your nearest stockist you may find that for several approaches to main ports there are specially enlarged charts. Charts now are not marked in fathoms (six feet to a fathom) but in metres and are coloured to differentiate between land, tidal areas and shallow and deep water.

With the first chart that you buy I recommend you also to buy the booklet that explains what the abbreviations and symbols mean on a chart. It is Booklet No. 5011 and isn't very expensive. You need the booklet because charts tell you far more than the depth you can expect. They describe the bottom with abbreviations like Ms—mussel, S—sand, M—mud, Sh—shells, etc. They also combine the symbols on mixed ground so that SbkSh would mean sand, broken shells. The charts also give you all the buoys, describing what type of a buoy it is, how often the lights on it flash (useful at night). Particularly strong tidal flows are marked with speed and direction.

It is difficult to suggest what type of ground to look for on a chart to find cod because they can gather on the whole range of bottoms according to where their food is. The only tip I can give is: don't believe that the deeper the water, the bigger the cod. Remember that cod will be found where their food is found, and that often means surprisingly shallow water. The rising edge of a bank can be a good spot, and you can locate this by a very modest echo sounder.

A word of general advice on gear: carry it in a haversack that can be easily stowed away under a seat. Baskets and boxes just get in the way with a small boat. You can also put all the spare gear anyone is likely to need into one bag.

The method of actually fishing from a boat doesn't vary

with either a small boat or a charter boat. There are countless ideas on what constitutes the best cod trace, but while many different designs are equally effective, I have stayed for a long while with the running leger type. Figure 13 shows how to tie it up. The weight is fastened to a clement boom with the reel line passing through the two eyes of the boom. The boom is stopped by tying on a swivel (I prefer large Berkley brand). A 3 ft. length of line the same strength as the reel line is tied to the other end of the swivel. A foot below the swivel, tie into this hook length a small blood loop and to this loop a length of line between six and eight inches long. Tie a hook to each end of the two pieces of line and the trace is made up. Do not make the short dropper length any more than eight inches or you will get excessive trouble with this hook spinning round the other. When using fish baits for big cod, I just have the one hook—no dropper.

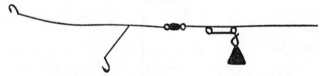

FIG. 13. This is my basic fishing rig. The weight is attached by means of a sliding Clement boom, stopped by a large swivel. The long hook length is between two and three feet long. The short dropper is no more than six inches from the main line about a foot from the swivel.

This rig works well for fishing at anchor, but if you prefer to try drifting—and I think more should—the trailing hooks tend to snag up too easily on the bottom. Instead, I use a rig tied up (as in Figure 13) using two French booms, with the lowest hook just missing the bottom. If you are drifting over broken ground, you can attach the weight to the rest of the tackle by a very short, weak length of line, so that if the weight does fasten, you lose only the weight and not the whole lot. To attach the French boom to the main line, all you have to do is to coil the line round the back wire of the boom (as shown in Figure 14) enough times to prevent it slipping down. The complete set of drift gear is shown in Figure 15.

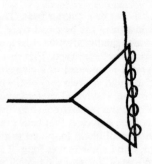

FIG. 14. The method attaching a French boom to the tackle.

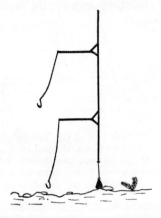

FIG. 15. My drift fishing tackle. French booms are used to stand the two-hook snoods off the main line. Note that the bottom hook is set to just miss the sea bed. The weight is attached by a six-inch length of much weaker line so as to break away easily should the weight get lodged during the drift.

The advantage of drift fishing is that you can cover a lot of ground, searching out the cod rather than waiting for them to come to you. If you are anchored over a barren piece of sea bed, you can wait all winter and the cod will not come. If you fish on the drift, however, soon you will pass over the barren bit of sea bed onto a part that holds fish. Keeping on the move in boat fishing is as important as in shore fishing.

There is another method of boat fishing for cod that has gained a lot of attention in recent years, called "boat-casting". The name is new but not the principle. However, much of the credit of re-popularising this method must go to the South East of England.

You need a rod between 8 ft. and 10 ft. long. Longer than that is not necessary and becomes cumbersome. The purpose of having a longer than normal rod is because you have to cast the tackle just as if you were on dry land. For this reason you also require a reel that will allow you to make a good, smooth cast. Heavy boat reels are out.

The single-hook rig I suggested for shore fishing is suitable, but you must have a good anchor lead on. You cast uptide of the anchored boat as far as you can. As soon as the weight hits bottom, keep on releasing line until the anchor bites and holds firm. You will have a very large bow in your line and the rod tip will set over in an arc. When the cod takes the bait and makes a run with it, it meets the resistance of the anchor dug firmly into the bottom and the sudden jerk sets the hook. As the cod pulls at the weight, it should release it from the bottom, sending it trundling along the bottom and releasing the tension on the rod tip.

When you see the rod tip lose that arc and go slack, you know that a fish has taken. It doesn't always work that simply, as the weight sometimes releases itself, giving false bites. The method is good where you are boat fishing in an area of heavy tide run, but will not work in very deep water. I can't give a maximum depth for this rig, but you can soon discover if you are in too much depth. The reason it will not work in deep water is that by the time the weight hits bottom it will have been swept back down the tide to almost underneath you.

To avoid having to use very heavy anchor leads, keep your line diameters low—18 lb. is plenty heavy enough. You need an anchor lead just heavy enough to hold bottom so that it will release easily when a cod takes the bait.

Lure Fishing

The growth in popularity of lure fishing has probably been the biggest single step forward in the art of catching cod since the modern beach-casting rod. The lure has become the aspirin for all those boat anglers with a bait headache, not as

93

a substitute for bait but as a method that will compete with and even beat a bait. The lure has been the downfall of many, many big cod, and it's a fair assumption that a lot of those cod would have been wandering the ocean still but for the lure.

Apart from solving the bait problem, the lure has proved to be a way of sorting out the better sized fish from a shoal. Large cod feed extensively on whole fish, and faced with the choice of a couple of lugworms and what appears to be a wounded fish, the big cod will go for the lure. Neither is lure fishing restricted to heavyweight lures. The small 2 oz. and 3 oz. versions of the larger lures fished on 20 lb. class tackle, even 12 lb. class if tidal conditions will allow, can give great fun.

Yet in spite of the success of lures (and there must be few boat anglers who don't possess at least one), there is still a widespread feeling that the lure comes second to bait in catching ability. This mistrust is perpetuated by the way in which many anglers use lures. When the fishing is poor and baits are catching little, on goes the lure and with great gusto it is heaved up and down for ten minutes or so. If baits are not producing any cod, it is reasonable to suppose there aren't any about, so the lure fails to catch. An angler who would happily wait a couple of hours for a take on bait, loses faith in a lure in minutes.

There is only one cure for this lack of faith and that is to have a good bag of fish on a lure. Once you've proved to yourself that lures really *do* work, you are converted for life.

The choice of lures on the shop counter is dazzling—literally. From tiny 1 oz. mini-fish to huge 2 lb. and over lures that look more suited to clubbing the cod rather than catching it. There is an equal array of colours and shapes. So much choice, in fact, that it becomes difficult to know what to buy.

That well-worn cliché of some lures being out to catch fishermen rather than fish is very apt. The fancy colour schemes and meticulous detail in the painting is totally un-necessary for cod lures. Irrespective of how poorly or well-developed the colour vision of a cod is in a laboratory tank, in the murk where most anglers seek them, it must be vir-tually impossible to tell colours. Don't be misled by television films and photographs where the colours seem nice and bright, because most of this footage is shot using banks of underwater floodlights. If you want to know how difficult colour recognition is in deep and dirty water, ask a skin diver, and remember that he is looking with the well-developed human eye. The easiest thing to see is the shiniest, which reflects what light there is down below.

But I don't even believe that vision plays a large part in persuading a cod to take a lure. In the cod biology section I talked of the echo sounding and radar ability of the lateral line, and I am reasonably convinced that this is the prime method a cod uses to home in on a lure. Vision comes in only in the closing stages. I cannot think of any better finish to a lure than chrome.

Oddly enough, the most common colour you find on a lure is red, which is the first colour to disappear as you go down through sea water. At around 40 ft., red turns to a dirty brown colour even in clear water. Other colours gradually fade with increasing depth and while they never quite reach the black and white stage, they all tend to look brownish. Ask any skin diver.

The correct way to work a lure is to touch the surface of the water with the tip of the rod and have just enough line out so that at this low point you can just feel the lure bump the sea bed. Then lift the rod smartly to the hoizontal position, wait until you feel the lure pull on the line, then lower the tip as the lure descends. This way you keep in constant contact with the lure. Should a fish take at any stage of the lure's rise or fall, you will feel it and be in a position to strike.

It is unnecessary to lift the rod any higher than the horizontal position when pirking. You will get quite enough action and lift into the lure from that one sharp movement. If you heave the rod over your head and a fish takes at the top of the stroke, you have nothing left with which to strike, besides which you will get tired quickly.

There is some disagreement over the need to strike when pirking. It is true that many cod are hooked either by their own snapping action, or while the lure is being lifted, but there are occasions when the hook has not been set, and without a sharp strike you would lose those fish.

There are two things that limit the action of a lure: the stretch in line and soft rod tips. Both have a cushioning effect which reduce by varying degrees the amount the lure moves. If you wish to use a light rod for lure fishing, you must use a light lure, particularly so in deep water. If you attempt to pirk with a heavy lure on a light rod, there will be insufficient power in the tip to lift the lure, and on each lift the tip will arc over instead of staying reasonably rigid. For this reason I also prefer to have a slightly longer rod than usual for pirking. The longer the rod, the more lift you will get. I like $7\frac{1}{2}$ ft. It is impossible to give a ratio for weight of lure to the pound class of the rod as it is closely governed by the depth you are fishing in and the stretch in your line. But if the tip arcs over excessively when you lift the lure, use either a heavier rod or a lighter lure.

We come now to the shape of the lure. I think all lures can be classified into two types: the flutter lures and the fast-droppers. The typical fluttering lure is the Abu Egon, a weighted, flattened tube bent over at an angle. When it falls through the water it does so with a fluttering action. Typical of the fast-dropper type are the bar pirks and those cast in the shape of a fish like the Abu Sillen.

The main difference in the two types is the speed at which they can be worked. An angler using a fast-dropping lure can get two lifts in the time it takes an angler using the slow-dropping flutter lure to do one. I think there is more action with the fluttering lure and consequently more vibrations being transmitted, but when it comes to the catching ability of the two types there doesn't seem to be any difference. If I had to sway one way it would be towards the fluttering lure . . . but only just.

The choice of lure size and weight should not be determined by the size of the cod you hope to catch. There is no evidence to suggest that big cod go for big lures in preference to smaller ones. The right weight of lure is the one that will produce the most action in the speed of tide in which you are fishing.

Because of the construction of the pirk, particularly so with fluttering lures, no matter what the weight, they will fall through the water with a weaving action, but you will get a greater action if the tide is allowed to move the lure as well as its own action. The other consideration on the choice of weight is tide drag on the line. Tide drag on the line is what causes the lure to ride up from the bottom and the two factors that control line drag are the speed of the tide and diameter of the line. It is essential that you feel your lure bumping on the bottom as this tells you that you are working at the right depth. If the lure continually rides up the tide, forcing you to keep paying out more line to find the bottom, increase the weight of your lure.

Any stretch at all in line when lure fishing is a bad thing. Using monofilament in reasonably shallow water is tolerable, but when you begin to fish in depths of over 100 feet, too much of the lift is cushioned, even with the best low-stretch lines. In deep water braided Terylene or Dacron is infinitely superior. Braided lines have virtually no stretch whatsoever, so whatever you lift with the rod on the surface is how much the lure will move fathoms below.

The drawback with braided lines is that their diameter is greater than for monofilament of comparable breaking strain, so you end up having to fish a lure heavier than you would have to do with monofilament. But being in firm contact with lure even in very deep water more than compensates. What is more, if you are using expensive shop-bought lures, I advise you to use line in the 50 lb. range. Unsporting it might be, but it makes sound economic sense. The very nature of lure fishing demands that the lure is constantly dropping on the bottom, and if you are fishing over broken ground, getting constantly snagged up is an occupational hazard.

But to get the maximum fun out of lure fishing, never turn down an opportunity to fish really light. There is no greater enjoyment I assure you.

What is the right time to use a pirk? Obviously when the cod are feeding. I said earlier that a lot of anglers only turn to pirking when they fail to catch cod on baits, which is grossly unfair. It isn't unusual for cod to follow predictable feeding habits, i.e. first of the flood, last of the ebb. There isn't a universal rule, but certain cod grounds have states of the tide when experience tells you if the cod are going to feed at all, it is then. So that is the best time to pirk.

But if you are on strange ground or experience says there isn't a best time, it's just random, then you have to stick it out and keep quietly working away. By all means have a rest now and then, but perseverance is a corner-stone of success with lure fishing. You have to be prepared for the cod suddenly to decide to take, and possibly only take for a short burst. If a few of you are working lures, always make sure that at least one angler is working, so that should the cod suddenly appear, they won't pass you by without your knowledge.

If you were bait fishing you would think it quite reasonable for an hour to pass without a bite, so be prepared to have an hour's lure fishing without anything.

Lures don't work in dirty water or at night. These two popular arguments are really saying the same thing, and they are both nonsense. Lures do work where visibility is nil. Recall my argument that vibration is the main attractor, not sight. In an identical situation I don't believe you will catch as many cod in darkness as in the same spot in daylight because in the final swoop, sight does play a part, but I've still had some darn good catches at night.

But the biggest aid of all in lure fishing comes from the heart, not from the tackle shop. It's called confidence. Without it you'll never really enjoy lures, you'll continually be wondering if a bunch of lug would be better. Stick at it though, waiting for that bumper day that will convince you for life.

Making your own lures

If you have the equipment and the ability, you can make lures just as efficient as the best shop-bought ones. When there is a perfectly good manufactured item, I don't see any point in making my own, so for normal fishing I use bought lures. But there is one occasion when I wouldn't be without my home-made lures and that is for wreck fishing. Especially when fishing on the drift over a few thousand tons of barnacle encrusted superstructure, the losses can be frightening. The best (or worst) figure I've ever known is eighteen lures lost by one angler on one trip. But the party had gone prepared for such losses, and they had spent many hours sawing up prams and touring scrap yards for car door handles. Imagine the cost of that fishing trip if those lures had been bought over the shop counter.

There are also those who find great pleasure in making their own tackle and would prefer to make their own than to buy lures. And the last category is the not-so-well-off, the young, who cannot afford to carry a full range of lures for all occasions. For these circumstances and people I'll explain DIY methods.

There are only two basic materials from which I make my own lures—chrome tubing and solid lead bar. I do not like materials like car door handles for lures because they are too light for their bulk. Chrome tubing is not difficult to obtain. You can tour round general dealers looking for it on old prams, bath-rails, etc.

The tubing is used for making fluttering lures, though you can also make bar pirks from it. The lead bar may be a little more difficult to obtain, but the shape you want is something that is no longer than six inches (or able to be cut down to that length). If you have difficulty in getting hold of lead bars, you can hammer flat lead piping, or alternatively pour molten lead into one of those large metal tubes that some cigars are sold in. When cold you can peel away the outer casing with pliers.

I do not like long lures. If you have a long lure, the cod could grab the pirk across the middle or towards the opposite end to where the hook is, and you will miss the cod. This grabbing broadside on, by the way, is the reason why in lure fishing you sometimes find the hook is fastened to the outside of the mouth instead of the inside. You haven't foul-hooked the fish—it's just characteristic of the way in which cod sometimes attack a small fish.

Six inches is the longest lures should be, and by using tubing of varying diameter you can have lures of over a pound at this length. Prams provide a narrow tubing ideal for four and five ounce lures, but to have a lure of eight ounces in the flattened style of a fluttering lure, you will need a diameter of around one inch, and you could have difficulty in finding that as cheap scrap. If all else fails, you will be able to buy the large diameter chrome tubing at a plumbers' merchants— it is used for shower-rails, etc.

To actually make a lure, cut off five inches of chrome tubing. Nip flat the last half inch, ideally in a big vice, but careful hammering will do it. Secure the tube in an upturned position (again a vice is ideal) and pour in sufficient molten lead to make the weight of lure you want. With pram tubing ($\frac{5}{8}$ in. diameter) you get 2 oz. of lure per inch of lead. With one inch diameter tubing you get around $3\frac{1}{2}$ oz. per inch. However, you can work it out for yourself using the kitchen scales.

If you wish to have a fast-dropping, heavy lure, you can fill up the tube to within $\frac{3}{4}$ in. of the top. When the lure is cold, nip the top flat as with the other end and drill a $\frac{1}{16}$ in. hole approximately $\frac{1}{8}$ in. from the edge on each flat surface.

Pass a big strong split ring through each hole, and a 4/0 treble fastens to one ring and the line to the other. It is unnecessary to use a swivel between the lure and the line, but if you wish to, I recommend the Berkley swivels.

To make a lure with a fluttering action, only half-fill the tube with lead (so to make heavy fluttering lures you will have to use larger diameter tubing). Hammer flat all the tubing that has not been filled with lead, then bend this flattened part over at an angle. According to the angle at which you bend the tube, you will get a slight or exaggerated action. The ends are flattened and drilled as the ordinary bar lures are. If the tubing you have is mild steel conduit tube, which has a seam in it, you may find that it will split to some degree during the flattening process. This does weaken the metal, but nothing like enough to present any danger with the strength of fishing lines even the most heavy-handed anglers use.

Beware of drilling too close to the edge of the flattened ends, or you will create a weak spot that could break. If you drill too far away from the edge, you will have difficulty in attaching the split ring.

To make solid lead lures, which are of the fast-dropping type, using a hacksaw and file, simply shape the bar of lead into something resembling a fish. There are then two ways you can get a reflective finish. Using a good waterproof adhesive, completely cover the lure, giving it a couple of coats to make the surface of the lure really tacky. Then roll the lure in a plastic bag with glitter particles in. The glitter dust is obtainable from most good hobby and handicraft shops. You can get different colours if you wish, though I don't think there is anything to beat the silver glitter.

Alternatively to dusting with glitter, buy a roll of chrome tape and wrap it tightly round the lure, pressing it into the lead. To stop the tape falling off, coat it all over with clear glue.

When you drill lead lures to make holes for the split ring, be especially wary of going too near the edge, for lead is a much softer material than chrome tubing and a narrow piece could easily snap off. During use, watch lead lures constantly for wear at this point, even on those you may have bought. At the first sign of weakness, drill another hole further up the bar.

Feathering

Feathering is probably the oldest form of lure fishing there is. Although these days feathers have been relegated to the lowly task of catching mackerel, the history of feathers for catching sea fish goes back hundreds of years.

I do not like the type of hook many feather tiers use on tackle shop feather flights. They are the tinned, spade-end hook with a monstrous barb. I wouldn't use them on the shore so I won't use them on a lure. I tie up my own feathers for cod fishing, using feathers I find, though if you have difficulty in getting white feathers (the colour I prefer) just walk into a poulterer's shop and ask to buy a few chest feathers of a white bird. Odds are on he will give them to you if you explain what you want the feathers for.

I use stainless steel 3/0 hooks, stainless so that the hooks won't rust up between use. I tie a good cluster of down feathers to the shank, and use just three feathers per flight, fastening them on snoods of heavy line just a couple of inches long.

There is an even simpler way than this of making feathers, and that is to dispense with real feathers altogether and just fold over a two inch piece of chrome Sellotape over the hook shank, with about half an inch trailing off the hook.

The wet feather is meant to imitate a small bait fish like whitebait or brit, and nothing flashes more realistically than a strip of chrome tape.

I wouldn't claim feathering to be a first choice method of catching cod, but it is especially worth setting up a flight if you get among a shoal of small to medium-sized codling, putting a lure on the bottom hook instead of a plain weight.

You can, of course, tip the feathers with a piece of bait—a small worm or a piece of fish. It appears that fishing in this way is neither one thing or the other, but it works, so you can't knock it too hard. But again, it has worked best in my experience with small codling.

Other Lures

There are two types of lures that you cannot group into either of the types already mentioned, so I'll put them together here at the end of the section. They are the baited spoon and the rubber eel.

The baited spoon is a method very rarely used seriously in cod fishing, and its exclusion is understandable considering the existing variety of methods already practised, but because it is little used, don't think it isn't much good. If you can gauge the circumstances right, the baited spoon can be a deadly way of fishing.

The first time I saw an Abu Rauto spoon used, the angler who used it latched into a cod of 43 lb. When his next cast produced one of 35 lb. and I was still only finding fish in the 12–15 lb. range, I thought it time to take a closer look at the spoon.

There are two schools of thought about why the baited spoon catches cod. The first is that the cod picks up the vibration of the spoon, sees it flash, and its curiosity sends it over to find the source of the disturbance. It finds a nice piece of food and takes it. The other idea is that the spoon works when the cod are bloated out with food. At times when natural feed like sprat, shrimp or sand-eel are plentiful, the cod are disinclined to take big baits because physically they can't manage any more. But they see and feel a flashing spoon, and possibly through bad temper as much as curiosity, move over to snap at what is causing the disturbance. The cod sees a piece of food, not a huge lump of fish which it couldn't possibly manage, but a tiny morsel. Rather than let it go, the cod snaps the tiny piece of bait up. You or I couldn't manage a steak right after a seven-course banquet, but we'd find room for a nice little piece of Stilton.

Both ideas sound reasonable, but both rely on the angler moving the spoon frequently to keep up the vibrations. A good way of fishing with a spoon is to use it in conjunction with a steel paternoster, tied on a short snood. Lift the tackle up and down in the tide almost continually. You will probably have to modify the spoon by increasing the line strength and the hook size, as most are designed primarily for catching flatfish.

The rubber sand-eel is something I've had great fun with for catching cod. I would never describe it as a deadly method, but it's so different from the way cod are normally caught from a boat that it is very pleasurable. There is no better eel than Alex Ingram's Red Gills. I think the long-vaned tail has a lot to do with it. If you hold one in a current, the tail wiggles away sending vibrations in all directions.

To tackle up with an eel, use a French boom and attach the eel by at least eight feet of line. This very long length allows the eel greater freedom of movement. The stronger the current you fish in, the better will be the action of the eel, in fact with very little current the eel won't have any movement at all. Apart from cod, there are many other sea fish that will go for an eel in this way. To get a fish in, you reel the tackle to the rod tip, then handline the long trace to the side of the boat.

Catching a big cod

It's never been a burning ambition of mine to catch a record cod. If it were and I deliberately set out to catch one to beat the current record of 53 lb. and succeeded, then I would feel some pride in achieving my declared goal. But most records —for cod in particular—have been broken by anglers who just did what they would normally do, and the achievement that comes without effort gives me little pleasure.

If you tackle up and fish in a manner that you expect will catch cod in the 3–5 lb. range and you get one of 10 lb., it's nice, but it isn't anything to shout about. You got lucky, that's all. My pleasure comes in succeeding at the type of fishing I set out to do, whether it's to catch spring two-pounders from a shingle beach, or haul up double-figure heavyweights from fifty fathoms.

If I were solely interested in large cod, I would never move away from the Firth of Clyde, where not only is there a great number of cod, but a great number of very large cod. There can't be any other place that produces so many double-figure cod every week-end, and for anyone whose pleasure is measured in pounds of flesh, there isn't anywhere finer.

Eric McVicar, has taken fourteen cod of over 40 lb. from the Clyde, three of which I've witnessed, and innumerable cod of over 30 lb. Large cod are all Eric is interested in and anything less than 20 lb. he treats with contempt. The first time we fished together I brought up a cod of 32 lb. from the wreck of the *Akar* on the Dunoon Bank. Big cod was what we had gone for and I thought I had succeeded. For Eric it was just a nice fish. Not until half an hour later when he latched into one of 42 lb. did he get excited.

If you set your sights purely on big cod you are going to miss out on a lot of fun. There is as much skill in taking small spring codling at 100 yards range on 12 lb. line as dragging a forty-pounder up through forty fathoms. In fact, I reckon there's a lot more skill with the springers.

The saddest case I've witnessed of big cod fever was with a fifteen-year-old schoolboy who has access to the big cod marks in the Clyde. He complained bitterly to me that while all his pals could catch cod of over 30 lb. he was pestered with twenty-pounders. And he was genuinely annoyed. Never let yourself become obsessed with the search for big cod.

Having warned of the dangers of catching big cod, I know a lot of anglers would like to tuck at least one big cod under their belt, if only to say they've done it.

Apart from location, the biggest problem is finding a bait that will be tempting to a big cod but not so appealing to small ones. Normally, successful cod baits such as crabs and worms are an obstacle to catching big cod because they are so readily snapped up by smaller fish.

I can give a personal example of this. One day we were fishing over a known big cod mark in the Clyde. There were three of us, one man fishing with peeler crab, one with a big lure and myself with a half mackerel. The pal with the peeler crab got fish after fish. Every time he hit bottom there was a cod banging away. He filled a fish box with cod of 4 lb., 6 lb., 8 lb., and even 9 lb.—but not one that went into double figures.

I didn't get half as many as he did with his crab, but I didn't get one under 15 lb. either. The man pirking fared similarly to me. There was a wide range of cod feeding below us from small to very large (we had six of over 30 lb) but the choice of bait was sorting out the sizes.

I suggest, then, that you think big when you are after big fish. Present a bait that seems too much for a small fish to manage and while you may not catch as many as the smaller bait angler, you stand a better chance of finding the bigger fish. As the example I've just given shows, a large fillet of fresh fish or a whole fish, dead or alive, such as a whiting or pouting, is far more effective than a couple of lug or a lump of peeler crab.

I have included this chapter on big fish in the boat fishing section because the best way of finding large fish is from a boat. Big cod are caught from the shore, but if you want to set your sights purposely on a big cod, I suggest you get afloat. But as I said at the beginning of this chapter, don't ever think that big is beautiful—it's not. The credit is in catching what you set out to catch.

CHAPTER FIVE

The Tail End

Having ploughed your way through this book you might be tempted to point out that you've got a good rod and reel, you know how to cast, you always dig your own bait, but you *still* aren't getting your share. I know lots of competent anglers who have this problem. They put far more hours into the search for cod than I do, but don't get much to show for it. If this is your problem, then you are suffering from lack of co-ordination. Putting all your accumulated skills into the right order.

I'll give you an example of what I mean. You have first class tackle and know how to use it. You get the best bait you can and plenty of it, then go down to the beach in the middle of the day when everyone knows that night is the only time to go to that spot.

Or maybe you get down to the beach at the right time and the cod are just queuing up to be caught. But you're trying to catch them with an old piece of herring while everyone else has a bucket of lug. In both cases you've got most of it right, but not all. The days when you could catch cod in spite of self-imposed handicaps are gone. You have got to get it all right.

Timing is particularly important. You have to go fishing not when it suits you but when it suits the fish. Sunday afternoon might be the most convenient time to go cod fishing for you and I, but is it for the fish? This is why club trips to distant beaches often end in disaster. How can you plan where to go and catch cod two months in advance when it might not be possible two days before?

Get your bait right, too. If you take along the bait that is second best on the beach you are fishing, what can you expect but second-best catches? It might take a lot of effort to get the best, but isn't it worth it in the end?

Another common fault is in expecting the cod to catch themselves. Getting everything right but being too idle to hold your rod or to watch the tip for bites. It's good to yarn to pals while fishing, but don't neglect the thing that has brought you down to the beach in the first place. Chat by all means, but do so with your rod in your hand ready to hit the bites when they come.

Which beach to go to is also important. Cod are widely distributed around the shores of Britain but they are not everywhere. If a beach has the reputation of being a poor cod beach, it has most likely earned that reputation the hard way, but there never seems to be a shortage of anglers trying earnestly to prove a reputation wrong.

If your local beach is a poor cod beach, accept the fact and be prepared to travel. I've always believed it better to travel an hour more and fish an hour less if that means you are going to get better fishing. Don't go cod fishing with the thought "you never know", because deep down you *do* know.

That's really all I have to say. Good fishing.

Index